MAN'S SPIRITUAL REALITY

The Spirit Man

{GEN1:26-27; 2:5-7}

BRO. CALEB F. IWORIE

BLUEPRINT PRESS
INTERNATIONALE

Man's Spiritual Reality
Copyright © 2023 by Bro. Caleb F. Iworie

ISBN
978-1-961117-02-0 (Paperback)
978-1-961117-03-7 (eBook)
978-1-961117-32-7 (Hardcover)

DEDICATION

This Book is dedicated to our Lord Jesus Christ for the furtherance of the Gospel.

TABLE OF CONTENTS

THE SPIRIT MAN GENESIS 1:26-27, GENESIS 2:7

OUTER INFLUENCES
(CARES OF THE WORLD)

As has already been told by the word of God; in this age of strong delusion that we have now seen among many apostate professing Christianity, God still has his people somewhere that He can point to and say, that's my people.

And we have often wanted to be among that class of people. I am certainly sure we all want to be there. This should be the expected desire of every heart. We want to be among that number that God can say, "This is my people! Look at them. They are an example of what I Am. They are truly reflecting My Life in theirs. They have surrendered their lives, and I am reflecting Mine Life through theirs." What a beautiful thing. How it must make God feel so good to know that He has gotten somebody somewhere that he can put trust in. Oh my!

Going further, WHY DID GOD SAY {you are going to be bamboozled why God said in the plural say...} "LET US" MAKE MAN IN OUR OWN IMAGE?

BRO. CALEB F. IWORE
Revised Edition

BOOK DESCRIPTION:

This masterpiece Book, MAN'S SPIRITUAL REALITY, [The Spirit Man} underpins the Origin of Mankind, and his destination back to God, as well as the much-needed insight into God's provided way of relating to man.

This Book has gone through phases, and has its first edition, titled "Who Is Born Again, as first published in 2017, but due to obvious reasons, was rebranded by the Page -Turner Press & Media, and now all the loose ends are tightened for our numerous readers around the globe with this updated title as MAN'S SPIRITUAL REALITY {The Spirit Man} by the Author Unit Media.

I am so glad that the dynamics and the mechanics of this revealed the hidden truth which now is made manifest to bring the true teaching to God's new and old converts and expound the knowledge of those who truly seek to know the truth at a time like this where there exists scarcity of the true teaching of the word of God.

The pictorial view of the cover page is a complete illustration of man's origin back to God. We trust that you will prayerfully and diligently get answers to knowing the basic fundamental truth of the Gospel by carefully studying this book. It's just amazing, incisive, and analytical!

We cannot truly talk about Man's SPIRITUAL REALITY without being Born Again as he only way back to God, and the mention of Nicodemus to whom this was spoken at the very beginning.

Now Nicodemus was a Pharisee at the top of his field. Not only is he a member of the Sanhedrin, but he was also the most renowned Bible teacher of his day, like we still have among us, the modern-day Pharisees of our time. Nicodemus watched the crowds as they listened to the Lord Jesus, and he knew he had never pulled the attention of an audience as Jesus does. Jesus spoke in simple terms, but His message up to this moment has great power. Being mesmerized by the life and things that Jesus had demonstrated, as he observed the miracles performed, knowing he has never performed even one miracle.

In spite of his achievements, in spite of his prominence in theological degrees, politics, culture, and religion, Nicodemus still acknowledged that he had a great need.

He realized that he needed to know God in the power of his resurrection!

AUTHOR'S NOTE:

MAN'S CELESTIAL BODY— THE THEOPHANY

"There is a NATURAL body, and there is a SPIRITUAL body.

And so it is written, the first man — Adam was made a living soul; the last Adam was made a quickening Spirit. The first man is of the earth, - **EARTHY**: and the second man is the Lord from Heaven. As is the earthy, such are they also that are earthy: and as is the HEAVENLY, such are they also that are Heavenly. And as we have borne the image of the Earthy, we shall also bear the IMAGE of the Heavenly. "

1. Cor 15:4449-.

"For we know that if our earthly house of this tabernacle were dissolved, we have a building of God, an **house not**

made with hands, eternal in the Heavens.
For in this we groan, earnestly desiring to
be clothed upon with our house which is
from Heaven".

2. Cor 5:1 -2.

"They also call that celestial body, a theophany, that when we leave this earthly flesh of our body here, we go into that glorified body. Whatever it may be, I take the apostle's Word, when he said, "If this earthly tabernacle or dwelling place {body} be dissolved, we have ONE already waiting to move from this flesh into that glorified body - theophany."

That celestial body is what is called our theophany. And as soon as the life leaves this earthly body, you go into that supernatural body, glorified body or body celestial. See? We have a body like God's glorious Body, the glorified Body of the Lord Jesus, raised up in that Image. When we see him, we shall be like him. Amen, that is the image of God that man is made up of, for God is a Spirit and He first created a spirit man in his likeness.

Now, theophany is a human body that is glorified, not exactly with flesh and blood like it will be in its glorified stage, but it is in a form of a human body that does not eat, neither does it drink nor does it have blood.

When Jesus was manifested in the Old Testament in a theophany, in the Person of Melchisedec, not a priesthood, but the Person, the Man... Oh hallelujah! For this Man had yet not been born, but He was in a theophany, so He had no Father, no Mother, no Decent. **He** is God Himself.

He manifested in the form of a Man called King of Salem, which is King of Peace and King of Righteousness. Oh my, my glorious amen! He was Melchisedec. Yes sir. He had neither Father nor Mother, no Beginning of Days and no Ending of Life. See? It was Jesus in his theophany form of a Man.

This is a great mystery by itself. And a "mystery" is Scripture, a previously hidden truth which its supernatural element still remains despite the revelation." Are you catching the revelation? Oh you better believe it!

You got to know who you are, where you came from, and where you are going back to. We are passing by on a journey through this earth. Someday and one of these days, if Jesus tarries, we are going back to our original abode. Are you ready?

PREFACE:

I am not such erudite of a known public writer, or a polished author; but from my simple humble heart, I am trying to evangelize and introduce the Lord Jesus Christ, who Is The Same Yesterday, Today, And Forever to every worthy seeker of the true gospel.

> ...How then shall they call on him in whom they have not believed? And how shall they believe in him of whom they have not heard? And how shall they hear without a preacher?

> Rom. 10:13-17.

It is upon this basic Christian principle that in this booklet, we intend to settle a few Salvation questions so we can know who truly has it.

> Reverently, let us remember the Word of our Lord, when He said to those Jews who believed on Him, if ye continue in my words, then are ye my disciples indeed; and ye shall know the truth and the truth shall set you free.

> Jn. 8:32.

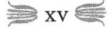

"But we speak the wisdom of God in a mystery, even the hidden wisdom, which God ordained before the world unto our glory:"

l. Cor 2:7.

With Salvation, then come **knowledge**, revelation and power, which are obtained for our own deliverance, from the clutch of sin. Salvation is the deliverance from the power and penalty of sin. Now works are fine, but works alone don't save you. I believe in godly conducts and character. If you have been truly saved, then you will literally crave to live righteously.

Now let me say it clearly, Salvation is not Jesus-plus. It is Jesus-alone FOR SALVATION IS OF THE LORD. From the start to the finish, it is all about GOD. Let His life be in me. His blood cleanses me from all unrighteousness. His Spirit fills me with power and glory. His Words in my heart and mouth set me apart for service or sanctifies me.

Now hear this testimony; "This day is salvation come to this house, forasmuch as he also is son of Abraham." Lk. 19:9. In here, the works of Zacchaeus showed his faith in our Savior Jesus Christ.

It was not the works of Zacchaeus that saved him. But it was his "faith" in Jesus Christ as the Savior. The "reaction to his faith" caused him to bring forth works meet for repentance".

Hallelujah amen!

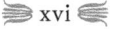

Therefore we need to work out our salvation with fear and trembling.

Phil 2:12.

Neither is there salvation in any other: for there is none other name under heaven given among men, whereby we must be saved.

Acts 4:12.

So many great men of old, have lived here on earth and made several boasts, and got many followers and converts till date.

But they all died and their bones still remain in the catacombs.

But the Lord Jesus died and left us an empty tomb in His grave because he resurrected; He reigns, the government is upon His shoulders, and is alive forevermore! On Christ the Solid Rock I stand, all other grounds are sinking sand: my hope is built on nothing less than Jesus Christ and his righteousness; and because he lives, I can face tomorrow.

These and more give us a true glimpse of what we intend to present in this book materials.

THE FALSE HUMAN EVOLUTION STORY

Notice, man is a spontaneous creation of God, and not the false and misleading evolution theory that gives credence to human evolving from an apelike descents that lived on earth a few million years ago.

This fiction is one of the greatest lies of Science, alluding that man evolved alongside orangutans, chimpanzees, bonobos, and gorillas. That all of these with man, share a common ancestoral leanage before about 7 million years ago. What a lie, what a blasphemy so deceitful?

But hear the gospel truth, if anything, man is a spontaneous creation of God.

But as we read from the account of Genesis that same teaching of man's evolution is not only illusive, but deceptive from the pit of hell.

Now trending from the account of God's word in Two scriptural quotes Genesis 1:26-27 and Genesis 2:5-7 will unravel the reality right here.

> And God said, LET US MAKE MAN IN OUR IMAGE AFTER OUR LIKENESS: AND LET THEM HAVE DOMINION OVER THE FISH OF THE SEA AND OVER THE FOWL OF THE AIR AND OVER THE CATTLE AND OVER ALL THE EARTH AND EVERY CREEPING THING THAT CREEPETH UPON THE EARTH.

> [5]And every plant of the field before it was in the earth, and every herb of the field before it grew: for the LORD God had not caused it to rain upon the earth, and THERE WAS NOT A MAN TO TILL THE GROUND.

> [6] But there went up a mist from the earth, and watered the whole face of the ground.

> [7]AND THE LORD GOD FORMED MAN OUT OF THE DUST OF THE GROUND, AND BREATHED INTO HIS NOSTRILS THE BREATH OF LIFE AND AND MAN BECAME A LIVING SOUL.

Now we got to use scriptural questions to secure scriptural responses with special reference that

God is a Spirit. Read on!

From these scriptures, you would notice that GOD CREATED MAN IN HIS OWN IMAGE AND IN HIS OWN LIKENESS, but the salient question we need to ask is: WHAT KIND OF A MAN DID HE CREATE? HE CREATED A SPIRIT MAN? Because reading down to Genesis 2:5 it says, THERE WAS NOT A MAN TO TILL THE GROUND. {Here we found God made a spirit man first according to Genesis1:26-27} an amateur God. In his own image

Now, if you'll notice, after He had made all the creation, God gave dominion of the cattle and the fishes and everything to the man. But, in His making up there, He made man in His own image to lead the cattle, lead the beasts of the field, just like the Holy Spirit leads the believer today, see.

In other words, Adam, the first man in the lower creations of God...

THE FIRST CREATION WAS GOD HIMSELF, GOD; THEN OUT OF GOD CAME THE LOGOS, WHICH WAS THE SON OF GOD; THEN OUT OF THE LOGOS, WHICH WAS THE WORD ("In the beginning was the Word, the Word was with God, and the Word was God."

"And the Word was made flesh and dwelt among us."), out of the Logos came forth the man.

John 1:1 In the beginning was the Word, and the Word was with God, and the Word was God.

John 1:14 And the Word was made flesh, and dwelt among us, (and we beheld his glory, the glory as of the only begotten of the Father,) full of grace and truth

Now let's go back a hundred million years before there ever was a star, moon, or anything in the world. Before the beginning of times...

Now, there was a time when there was nothing here, it was just all forever eternity.

And all of Eternity is God; He was there before the beginning of time.

Notice, "No man has seen the Father at anytime." No man can see God in his bodily form, because God is not in body form; GOD IS A SPIRIT, see?

"No man has seen the Father, but the only begotten of the Father hath declared Him."

Now, but notice now. There is just Space! There's no light, there's no dark, there's no nothing, it just seems nothing. But in there is a Great Supernatural Being, the Self Existent Ancient of Days, who covered all space of all places of all times. He was from Everlasting to Everlasting, He is the Beginning of Creation. Oh, that's God! But He wasn't really God then. Because God is an Object of worship, decorated with unfolding titles. So He became God when He began to receive worship from his angels worship. He became Creator when he created the Heavens and the earth. He became the Creator. Genesis 1:1. See?

John 1:18 No man hath seen God at any time; the only begotten Son, which is in the bosom of the Father, he hath declared him.

Now, no one has ever seen God because He is a Spirit being. And now, the next thing we begin to see, by eyes of supernatural looking, we see white Light forming out there. What was that? That was called, by Bible readers, " the Logos," or "the part of God begin to develop into something so human beings could have some type of an idea what it was. It's a little light, moving. That was the Word of God. Oh glorious amen, amen!

Of a surety, man have direct evolution from God because GOD IS A SPIRIT and created a spirit man or an amature god! Man evoluted from God and not from a somewhat like ape, gorilla or chimpanzee as being claimed by scientists.

Now, in John 1, He said, "In the beginning was the Word, and the Word was God." "And the Word was made flesh and dwelt among us." God unfolding Himself, down to a human being.

Genesis 1:26 And God said, Let us make man in our image, after our likeness: and let them have dominion over the fish of the sea, and over the fowl of the air, and over the cattle, and over all the earth, and over every creeping thing that creepeth upon the earth.

[19]Now, but then there was no man to till the soil (Genesis 2), no man to till the soil. "And then God formed man" (Genesis 2:7) " out of the dust of the earth." He formed man out of the dust of the earth, and put this supernatural Spirit..

Now, he was laying there. I can have many pictures of it. I see Adam standing... Let's take this way: See him standing like a tree. God had made him. He was dead as he could be; his toes, like the roots, sticking in the ground. And God said, "Let there be,"... or, breathed the breath of life into him, and he jumped, came to himself.

He breathed the breath of life into him, he became a living soul. Now, he begin to move on, move on.

Genesis 2:7 AND THE LORD GOD FORMED MAN OF THE DUST OF THE GROUND AND THE LORD BREATHED INTO HIS NOSTRILS THE BREATH OF LIFE AND MAN BECAME A LIVING SOUL.

[20]And then God taken from his side a piece of him, a rib, and made a woman. Now, where did He get the spirit woman, see? Genesis 1:26: He said, "Let us make man in our own image, after our own likeness, created He them (man) male and female." He made the burly spirit for man; He made the tender, little, delicate, feminine spirit for the woman. AND WHEN YOU SEE A WOMAN ACTING LIKE A MAN, SHE'S JUST GOT OUT OF HER PLACE, YOU SEE, IN THE IN THE BEGINNING, IT'S A SHAME THAT WOMEN HAVE LOST THEIR DAINTY, FEMINISH PLACE. THE SAME THING GOES FOR A MAN GOT OUT OF HIS PLACE AND START ACTING LIKE A WOMAN.

IT'S A DISGRACE, IT'S A SHAME!

THE MOST HIDDEN TRUTH OF ALL AGES.

T here were many trees in the garden of Eden, including the tree of Life and the tree of the Knowledge of Good and Evil. The Fall was not caused by eating natural fruit, which was permitted, and nothing is recorded in Genesis 3 about eating an apple, we read only about partaking of fruit of the tree of Knowledge. Therefore, it is important for us to know who and what the tree of Knowledge was.

In Genesis 3:7 we read, "And the eyes of them both were opened, and they knew that they were naked: and they sewed fig leaves together, and made themselves skirts." Something terrible had happened. Satan's promise was half fulfilled but not quite as expected; they had developed a self consciousness of their nakedness and of the guilt of their genitalia, which hitherto had been public but which they now considered private and sought to hide from each another, and from the Lord. You will notice, they did not blindfold their eyes or cover their mouth, but veiled their guilty reproductive organs that instead of bringing life, had introduced death into the world. Guilt-conscious, their intimate relationship with God is replaced by distrustful, selfish, servile fear, as the first common act of sin passes over to a second, and they seek to hide themselves and their sin amongst the trees of the garden.

Genesis 3 portrays the lust of the eye, the lust of the flesh, and the pride of life. Every man and woman understands temptation of the senses, so Eve's admission, "the serpent beguiled me, and I did eat" should be understood by every adult person. When a girl or a boy is entrapped and beguiled, we know it was not an ice-cream or apple they ate.

The apostle Paul certainly knew what happened in the garden of Eden. Otherwise he could not have admonished the Corinthian church, "But I fear, lest by any means, as the serpent beguiled Eve through his craftiness, so your minds should be corrupted from the simplicity that is in Christ" (II Corinthians 11:3). In view of the Fall, the apostle writes further, "And Adam was not deceived, but the woman, being deceived, was in the transgression" {I Timothy 2:14}.

Directly after it happened, the Lord God told Eve, "I will greatly multiply your pain in childbearing; in pain you shall bring forth children..." {Genesis 3:16}. This statement tells us what really happened. It was not meals she was to eat in pain as one might suppose had the transgression been epicurean; and neither Adam nor yet any woman has conceived by just eating fruit.

God knew what took place, and where punishment should be pronounced. Therefore as a memorial of the original sin, and under normal circumstances, women give birth in pain. They don't suffer toothache at mealtimes.

Proverbs 30:18-20, "Such is the way of an adulterous woman; she eats, and wipes her orifice, and says, I have done no wickedness."

Birth-pains remind women of the original sin, " for the woman being deceived was in the transgression," and lost her co-equality with man {Genesis 3:16; I Timothy 2:8-15}. Under the Old Covenant, circumcision in the male organ of generation recognised that because of the Fall corruption is inherently transmitted by our sexual conception {Psalm 51:5}, and symbolised an Israelite man's severance from nature's defilement to a state of consecrated fellowship with God. Hereby an unmarried Israelite woman came under the Covenant by the token of her father, and a married woman came under the token of her husband {I Corinthians 11:3-16; Ephesians 5:20-23}. So "God's holy One, whose flesh should not see corruption" was "born of a virgin" {Psalm 16:10; Isaiah 7:14}. When God made a Covenant with Abraham and his natural seed He required circumcision, "This is My covenant, which you shall keep, between Me and you and your seed after you: every male child among you shall be circumcised" {Genesis 17:10-14}. Every soul who refused circumcision was "cut off" from His people because he did not have the token of the Covenant.

In Jeremiah 9:24-25 we read, "THUS SAITH THE LORD, the days are coming when I will punish all these circumcised with the uncircumcised; Egypt, Judah, Edom, the children of Ammon, Moab, and the Semitic Arabs who dwell in the desert and cut the edge of their beard: for all these nations are uncircumcised, and all the house of Israel are uncircumcised in the heart."

Three classes are distinguished here, the Covenant people, their Serpent seed half brothers, their Semitic Ammonite, Moabite and Arabian cousins, and Gentile Egyptians. All of these nations were uncircumcised in spite of a circumcision in the flesh, {which from Israel's standpoint was an unjustifiable imitation of the sacred sign of the Covenant}, while the whole house of Israel, including Judah, is uncircumcised in heart and ears and essentially no different from the heathen nations without the token. From this it is evident that the only means of escape from the threatened punishment is a living and truly productive knowledge of the Lord {Jeremiah 9:22-23}.

In Genesis 17:12-13 and Exodus 12:43-49 we learn that every Israelite and every Gentile of Adam's race must have the token of circumcision in the flesh before he can partake of the Passover, which the Serpent's seed are forbidden to eat. However John Hyrcanus compelled them to "circumcise their genitals, and make use of the laws of the Jews; and they were so desirous of living in the country of their forefathers, that they submitted to the use of circumcision, {25} and of the rest of the Jewish ways of living; at which time therefore this befell them, that they were hereafter no other than Jews".

Before one is fit to celebrate our "Passover," which is to partake the Lord's Supper and footwashing under the New Covenant, he or she must be circumcised—not in the flesh—but in heart and ears, and our Token, unlike that of the Israelite, must be on display for it is the Life of Christ generated by the Spirit of Christ within the individual believer. Whereas the Israelite woman was "saved" under the Token of her father or her husband, "the unbelieving husband is sanctified by the Token of his Christian wife, and the unbelieving wife is sanctified under the Token of her Christian husband" (I Corinthians, 7:11-19).

There is no shame in displaying our Token, and our Token is not the Token unless it is on public display. Now the soul that refuses the Message of God's Prophet in this day is "cut off" and "shall be destroyed from among the people" (Malachi 4:6; Acts 3:23; Revelation 22:17-19). This is so because since the Seven Seals are revealed, Christ is no longer a Mediator for ignorance, and without this Message he is "uncircumcised in heart and ears" and cannot have the Token, which is the new birth by the Fullness of the Word, aside from which he cannot be restored to fellowship with our Lord Jesus Christ who is the Word (Matthew 17:11; Acts 3:21-23; I Corinthians 13:10; John 17:20-26).

The Lord God pronounced judgment on the serpent for his wickedness and said, "Because you have done this, you are cursed more than all cattle and every beast of the field; upon your belly you shall go, and eat dust all the days of your life" (Genesis 3:14). Up to that time, the serpent walked upright, else the statement "upon your belly you shall go" would make no sense (Ezekiel 28:13-14).

Most important is the following verse, "And I will put enmity between you and the woman, and between your seed and her seed; he shall bruise your head, and you shall bruise his heel." According to the testimony of the Lord God, there would be two different seeds. He spoke of the seed of the serpent, and also of its archenemy, both seeds would come through the woman. In Scripture, seed speaks of offspring, and there were in Eve's womb two different seeds as there are two different seeds in the church.

Satan cannot beget nor can he create. He is a sexless, fallen spirit-being. Therefore he had to make use of the beast which was closest to man and could even speak. Only after the curse, did the serpent lose its upright human form and become a reptile.

Genesis three records the conversation between the serpent and Eve. It began with the well-known question, "Yea, has God said?" The devil always uses the same approach: planting doubts about God's Word. Thus he misconstrued It, and entangled Eve. "You shall not surely die... Your eyes shall be opened, and you shall be as gods, knowing good and evil." Uplifted at the prospect of teaching her husband the secret knowledge of sex — how they might fulfill God's Command to "multiply and fill the earth," Eve fell for Satan's lie. What benefit was this knowledge of good and evil that separated them from God's Presence? Since that time the eyes of each one of us have been opened to know good and evil whereby we are accountable to God (Romans 5:12-14).

The human attributes are found in the genes which actually lie in the chromosomes inherited through begetting in the sex act. In this way, Satan was able to inject his nature vicariously through the serpent into the human race in Cain and his lineage. Eve's transgression caused Adam to forfeit our dominion over earth to death. As we are conceived according to Satan's worldly wisdom, we are born with a nature of this world, which is the nature of the god of this evil age. Therefore the Redeemer had to come into human flesh "That through death He might destroy him that had the power of death, that is, the Devil, and deliver them who, through fear of death, were all their lifetime subject to bondage" {Hebrews 2:14-15}. Conquering Satan and death, and rising the third day, Jesus announced victoriously, "I have the keys of death and hell" {Revelation 1:18}.

God's commandment was, "Be fruitful, and multiply" (Genesis 1:28), so He instituted marriage and joined the first pair together. The tragedy lies in the breaking of this first marriage, when Eve listened to one she knew to be inspired by Satan, and in correcting him made God's prohibition even stronger by adding, "neither shall you touch the Tree of the Knowledge of Good and Evil," which is Satan. Hereby she usurped authority over her husband, who was the spoken Word of God. Every species was to bring forth after his own kind, but in Eve's womb was a creature, cross-bred from Satan through the serpent, and not in the original creation. Whatever does not derive from His thoughts can never submit to the Word of God, which is His thoughts expressed. Eve then gave herself to Adam.

Adam knew Eve was no more a virgin, and although she should have been burnt as says the law (which is forever written in heaven), he was not deceived, but he loved her and quickly took her to himself. Eve was dying, having crossed the Word from eternity into time but as a son of God Adam knew he could no more be lost than God can be lost. He also knew that Eve was part of him and if he joined her in death, God must somehow redeem him, so in dying he would 'save' Eve. A perfect type of Christ.

Thus, the Fall took place: Eve gave herself to the serpent, then had her first relation with Adam. From both unions, which happened in quick succession, children were born: Cain and Abel.

In this day, 'twins' are born of different fathers. The best-known cases happened in Sweden and France. In Stockholm, when Mrs. Bjoerlen gave birth on the same day to a black, and to a blond, blue-eyed baby, her husband refused to take financial responsibility for the child which clearly was not his. In the trial Mrs. Bjoerlen admitted to having a black lover. On the same day she had known both men. In France, a Mrs. Duval also gave birth to a white and a black child, and 26 year old Marseilles prostitute, Yvette Landru, gave birth to one white, one Negro, and one Chinese. Medical records are replete with cases of superfetation in humans, where a woman with multiple ovum is fertilized by sperm of separate insemination. The offspring are not truly twins but half-brothers or half-sisters. True twins result from simultaneous fertilization of one ovum by two sperm.

Whoever reads Genesis 3:15 carefully, will see the Lord God had spoken of the two seeds, or offspring right after the Fall. So from the very beginning, there were these two lineages: the ungodly line of Cain and the godly line found in Seth.

Not once is Cain mentioned in the genealogies of Adam in the Old or the New Testament. Not one time is Adam called the father of Cain. This is why Adam pronounced his wife "the mother of all living": never is it suggested that he is the father of all living (Genesis 3:20).

Had Cain been the first-born son of Adam, he would have had the nature of Adam who was the son of God, and a special place in God's record.

As Eve bore her firstborn, she exclaimed, "I have gotten a man from the Lord" (Genesis 4:1). This must be understood correctly. Eve was NOT declaring Adam was the father of Cain: under Satan's delusion she actually thought Cain was Christ, "the beginning of the creation of God." No other act with Adam is recorded between the births of Cain and Abel. We are simply told, "... And she again bore his brother, Abel. And Adam knew his wife again; and she bore a son, and called his name Seth..." (Genesis 4:25). Since THREE sons were born from TWO acts by Adam, you know POSITIVELY that ONE of those three was NOT the son of Adam.

The apostle John also knew what happened in the garden of Eden. He wrote, "... not as Cain, who was of that wicked one" (I John 3:12). In this statement Adam could never have been meant. Adam was not the evil one, neither the wicked one, whose son Cain was, according to the written Word of God. The same apostle wrote of the believers, "... because you have overcome the wicked one" (I John 2:13, 14). Again Satan is meant in this place as in many other places in the Scripture with this description.

In Revelation 20:2, he is called "the dragon, that old serpent, who is the Devil and Satan." In the Gospels Jesus calls the opponent of God "the wicked one." God is altogether good; Satan is just the opposite. In the Lord's prayer we petition, "Lead us not into temptation, but deliver us from the evil one" (Matthew 6:13). We now know "the evil one" is the vicarious father of Cain and origin of all ungodly things.

Cain, the first killer and murderer, was full of envy and jealousy; and Satan was a murderer from the beginning — not in heaven, but on earth (John 8:44). Now it behooves us to consider what prompted such envy and jealousy as would cause Cain to murder Abel. It arose from their worship of God. Cain was rejected with his revelation, because he was carnal.

Perhaps he thought it was an apple that caused the Fall, and knowing God requires life for life, picked the choicest of his crop, knowing the 'life' would go out of it. But by revelation from God the Bible says Abel knew animal had caused the Fall, and so animal life must be offered.

When the elder saw his 'works' rejected and Abel's sacrifice for which he had not labored, accepted of God, it seemed so unreasonable. And when God told him he would be accepted if by faith he offered the same sacrifice as His vindicated prophet, he felt humiliated. Concealing his pride, Cain asked Abel to expound the faith. Abel was reluctant to explain, fearing for his life, but when Cain prevailed he expounded the 'original sin.' Cain recognized he was not Adam's son, that he had never possessed the birthright, and was nowhere in the genealogy of God, but that if he destroyed Abel, he reasoned there was the possibility of fabricating primogeniture.

Hence, when God exposed Cain's evil and he saw there was no way he could claim Adam's birthright, which is ultimately the restoration to eternal Life in a restored world, he exclaimed, "... from Your face I shall be hid; and

I will be a fugitive and a vagabond in the earth; and it shall come to pass, that every one that finds me shall slay me" {because intermarriage with his line always procreates the unredeemable serpent seed and further pollutes the human race}.

So to prevent man from taking vengeance on Cain and his kindred, God placed a mark upon him. That mark is worldly wisdom: reasoning against the faith. According to anthropologists and Brother Branham, the serpent seed were responsible for all inventions and the discovery of all technological principles.

It is absolutely impossible for Cain to have come forth from Adam who was created in the image of the holy God from Whom no evil can come. Satan misused the serpent to enter into the human race in this cunning way, and throw it into destruction and death.

Thus it was necessary for God to come in human flesh without human male instrumentality to redeem us back from the power of Satan. When all the redeemed receive their full inheritance, we will be placed back into our original ordained position under God to rule over all the earth.

Enoch was the seventh from Adam: Cain was not counted in the genealogy (Jude 14). Abel was killed with no offspring, therefore the record of the genealogy goes through Seth. In this respect, the Word of God is also perfect and enlightening — Adam, Seth, Enos, Cainan, Mahalaleel, Jared, Enoch — Cain is not Adam's seed and is not mentioned (Genesis 5:6-18; Luke 3:38).

The seed of the serpent was just as real as the seed of the woman. If the serpent did not have a seed, then Christ too was a myth. The seed of the serpent was Cain, the promised seed of the woman was Christ. Paul referred to the promised seed, "... and to your seed, which is Christ" (Galatians 3:16-19). He is the seed for whom the promise was given. In the Old Testament, we read, "When You shall make His soul an offering for sin, He shall see His seed" (Isaiah 53:10). God's law states that every seed must reproduce after its own kind {Genesis 1:11}. So we should recognize not only did the serpent seed produce a physical race of people not on the Book of Life, but it also produces spiritual death in Adam's race, causing names to be removed from the Book of Life.

God hates hybreeding — His Word is Spirit, and it is Life, but when mixed with human reasoning it is no longer His Word and becomes death {John 6:63; Revelation 22:18-19}. In Luke 8:11 we read, "The seed is the Word of God." Before Eve could receive the physical seed of the serpent, she first had to receive the perverted word or suggestion of Satan into her mind - spiritual serpent seed and reason against the clear instruction of God's seed Word.

In Matthew 13:36-43 the Lord spoke clearly about these diverse spiritual seeds, "He that sows the good seed is the Son of man; the field is the world; the good seed are the children of the kingdom, but the tares are the children of the wicked one." Our lives manifest our faith or understanding. A LIFE LIVED BY THE WORD IS THE WORD EXPRESSED - Christ in you, the hope of glory. A life lived by God's Word hybrid into creeds is reasoning against the faith; it is the mark of Cain and of the beast, and is death.

Those influenced by the wicked one hardened their hearts, to which Jesus said, "You are of your father the Devil, and the lusts of your father you will do. He was a murderer from the beginning, and abode not in the truth, because there no truth in him." He did not dispute their claim to be Abraham's seed, nor did he concede that they were also the seed of Isaac and Jacob and therefore Israelites.

As we have noted, the majority of Judeans (or Jews) in His day were Edomites. Esau, their progenitor was Abraham's seed but he married into Cain's race and marred his inheritance. Knowing this the Pharisees protested, "We were not born of fornication; we have one father, even God." Jesus said, "If you were Abraham's children you would do the works of Abraham... and if God were your father, you would love Me." Since they were deceived on the Word and abode not in the Truth, even those who were in Adam's line physically, were serpent seed SPIRITUALLY, and blotted from the record of life (John 8:37-47; Psalm 69:21-28; Jeremiah 9:24-25).

We must remember that God put "enmity" between the two seeds, "And I will put enmity between... your seed and her seed" (Genesis 3:15). With the aid of the serpent, Satan came into the human race to destroy God's order. And the enmity is still there.

Satan perverted God's holy instruction to "multiply and fill the earth," deceiving Eve and coming into human flesh and blood to produce death instead of life. "Man that's born of woman is of few days, and full of trouble" (Job 14:1). God required a perfect substitute, so Jesus was born of a virgin without sex, by faith in the spoken Word

Seed of God to pay sin's penalty. Hence our second birth is not by woman but by the Man Christ Jesus without sin and without sex, by the spoken seed Word of God.

After Pentecost, Satan returned to pervert the spoken Word seed of God by mixing or hybridizing it with reasoning into creeds and traditions. So long as the seven-sealed Book was closed and the mystery sealed to the time of the end, Christ was in the Office of Mediator, interceding in behalf of the ignorance of God's elect concerning the faith (Daniel 12:4,9; Revelation 10:4,7). Once the last saint predestinated to the Laodicean Church Age had been baptized into the Body, Christ answered the call of the elders, fulfilling Revelation 4, 5, and 10:1-7.

Advancing from the sacrifice altar as the bleeding bloody Lamb and taking the Book of Life, which is the title deed to all He has redeemed, He became Lion, Judge, and King of Kings. Revelation 10:1-6 signifies Christ descending to earth in WORD Form with the Book that was sealed open in His hands to reveal Himself through the ministry of the 'angel' to the Laodicean Church Age before the seventh Trumpet Angel sounds the end of the Gentile Dispensation (I Thessalonians 4:16; I Corinthians 15:52).

You see the Church Age saints cannot be made perfect without us. As the Holy Spirit was waved before God in the first ripe Sheaf of the Lord Jesus Christ, and accepted in that God resurrected Him for the justification of the whole harvest (Romans 4:25), that same Spirit in the Fullness of the Word is to be waved again in the end-time Bride whose acceptance will signal the resurrection of the sleeping saints and build faith for translation grace. The "church" will know nothing of this: God having called out the righteous, both wise and foolish virgin, their end will be a lake of Fire (Leviticus 23:16-21; Matthew 3:12; I Thessalonians 5:1-10; Revelation 19:20; 20:10).

Speaking through His prophets, God promised He would "RESTORE the faith once delivered to the apostolic saints" (Joel 2:25; Malachi 4:5-6; Matthew 17:11; Acts 3:19-21). This is the ministry of the seventh Church Age Messenger, the prophet of Malachi 4:5-6, whose Message is the "shout" of I Thessalonians 4:16, which is the "midnight cry" heard and heeded by the wise and foolish virgin of Matthew 25:6 and confirmed by the heavenly Voice of Revelation 18:4. This Message is Christ the fullness of the Word "spoken by the mouth of all God's holy prophets since the world began" —"that which is perfect" or complete (Acts 3:21; I Corinthians 13:10; Revelation 10:7). It separates Christ's tiny Flock from the hordes of the great whore of Rome and her Protestant harlot daughters, bringing her into the unity of the faith for the manifestation of the Sons of God and the translation (Genesis 49:10; Amos 3:3; Matthew 13:41; Ephesians 1:10; Romans 8:19; II Thessalonians 2:1).

The 'enmity' God placed between the seed of the righteous first and last Adams, and the unrighteous physical seed of Cain and the bastard-born spiritual children of the second Eve, whom Jesus calls "the mother of harlots and abominations on the earth," is extant. Christ's little Flock is marching toward heaven in the rapture, while Satan's mighty world-wide church is marching to Armageddon (Revelation 16:13-16; 17:14).

Revelation 1-3 prophesies the battle that commenced on the day of Pentecost between Christ in His people, and antichrist in his people. These trees that stood in the midst of the Garden have grown together, like Judas and Jesus, as brothers within the framework of the Christian church, so close as would almost deceive the very elect if it were possible. However this is the harvest time, each congregation is bearing the life of the seed that was planted and cannot hide its fruit. Satan's apostate big church is uniting with the apostate smaller churches in order to convert or kill Christ's little Flock. But after a brief and powerful demonstration of the Spirit — NOT a public display as it was in Pentecost — our little hunted and persecuted group will go to be with Jesus.

As Satan incarnate the beast in the garden of Eden and led the first Eve to death, when he is cast out of the heavenlies he will evict his demons and incarnate the man of sin, thereafter called the beast, who will lead his followers to perdition. Christ's purpose is to be fulfilled in His Bride. He is that Corn of Wheat that fell to the ground at Calvary in order to reproduce Himself in the many-membered spoken Word seed Bride.

When Jesus was on earth, Satan showed Him all the kingdoms and their glory in this end-time and said, "I will give You all these things if You will fall down and worship me" (Matthew 4:9). Our Redeemer knew that once He overcame, and shed His blood for the redemption of those ordained for eternal Life, the inheritance forfeited by the first Adam would be His. Already the psalmist had said, "Arise, O God, judge the earth; for You shall inherit all nations" (Psalm 82:8; Revelation 11:15).

Of Christ's elect or Spiritual Seed, the apostle Paul wrote, "And if children, then heirs; heirs of God, and joint heirs with Christ — if so be that we suffer with Him, we may be also glorified together" (Romans 8:17). This will be fulfilled sooner than most (so-called) Christians dare imagine. We are privileged to live in the time when all the mysteries contained in the Holy Scriptures have been revealed, including the original sin in the garden of Eden.

Genesis 4 is intended to be a historical message. In verse one, the connection with what precedes is very clear. The history here recorded is tied to the Paradise narrative with the conjunctive phrase, "And Adam," or "And the man" Adam is presented as being familiar to us from the preceding events, with no further introduction necessary. Also, his wife is simply presented by her name, Eve, "mother of all living," which according to Genesis 3:20, she had been given by her husband following the Fall, whence Eve bore in her womb two seeds (Genesis 3:11-17).

This history traces the enmity God has placed between these two seeds and foreshadows the Promise. The writer must first dispose of Cain and his ungodly line who have NO part in the Promise or Kingdom of God. Then he returns to Seth through whom the line of Promise is maintained. The story of Cain and Abel points out that from the very first, men have been divided into two great classes, viewed in connection with God's Promise and Presence in the world.

Whilst it is to the self-reliant and God-defying energy of the descendants of Cain that we owe much of the external civilization of the world, the descendants of Seth pass away and leave only this record: that they "walked with God".

Genesis 4 is the historical account of the sinful misapplication of God's command in the garden, to "multiply and fill the earth" which produced DEATH by Eve's reasoning with Satan through the agency of the serpent, instead of awaiting God's uncompromised Word revealed through her husband in due season.

This is the first mention of a sexual relationship between Adam and his wife. Cain had already been conceived by the serpent prior to Adam having knowledge of his wife. Eve saw in Cain the fulfillment of the natural promise of Genesis 3:15, and looked on her first child as God Himself, the 'Deliverer', Who would restore them to Eden. It is unusual for the mother to justify Cain's name by declaring "I have begotten a "MAN" with the Lord," when Cain was but a babe. To Eve, however, Cain was the 'Man child' (Revelation 12:13) Who would smite the Serpent. Eve did not claim to bear Cain by Adam but supposed he was gotten, acquired, or created with the Lord.

It is NOT said of Eve that she conceived again and bare Abel (which is the usual Scriptural way of intimating a second birth) but simply that she bore him after Cain. That a difference was from the very first put between the two, is plain from the remarkable language which she applies to the firstborn, "I have gotten a man from the Lord;" and indeed from the very names given the two brothers respectively. Cain signifies 'acquired one' -- Eve was deceived by Satan who incarnate the Serpent, she and thought Cain was the

Son of God, whereas she KNEW Abel was the son of her own husband and named him accordingly.

Abel means 'a son', which well suits the first-born child of man. Hence we have the line of the serpent through Cain (falsely supposed to be the Son of God), and the line of Adam, beginning in Abel. The etymology of Cain and Abel are quite separate.

From their birth, at the same time, there was a difference put on these two sons of Eve. It was understood from Genesis 3:15, that the race was to be divided into two great sections, of which one only was to be reckoned as truly and spiritually the seed of the woman, while the other bore the character and fell under the doom, of the seed of the serpent.

Eve regarded her firstborn son as the very individual who was to be the Savior, and understood at the same time that this Savior was to be a divine person. Hence her words, "I have gotten a man" or 'the man', 'the Lord,' the very Jehovah -- Him who is God as well as man. Or, "I have gotten a man from the Lord." So Eve was STILL deceived at Cain's birth. But because "that which is flesh is flesh;" and born by sex, Cain was in need of redemption himself and could not possibly be the Redeemer (I Corinthians 15:45-49).

At all events, it is plain that in her judgment Cain was chosen rather than his comparatively lightly esteemed half-brother, whose very name in Hebrew means 'vanity,' or 'nothingness.' (Though of course, Adam and Eve did not speak Hebrew).

Like the spiritual serpent seed, (Adam's children deceived on the Word), and God's elect, these step-brothers, representatives of the two great classes into which, the family of man is divided, manifest their differences NOT in the object, NOR in the time, BUT in the spirit, of their worship. "And in the process of time it came to pass that Cain brought of the fruit of the ground an offering unto the Lord. And Abel, he also brought of the firstlings of his flock, and of the fat thereof" (Genesis 4:3-4).

Like the spiritual seed of the wicked one and the Holy One, the descendants of the serpent and of Adam both worship the same God, and receive the same anointing of His power and glory (Matthew 5:45; Acts 2:17). Their seasons of worship are also the same; for the expression "in process of time," or "at the end of days," denotes a stated season (corresponding with Passover). Again their manner of service was to a large extent the same. They presented offerings to God of two kinds, corresponding remarkably to the two kinds of offerings ordained under the Levitical dispensation -- those which were properly expiatory, and those which were mainly expressive of duty, gratitude, and devotion.

"By faith Abel offered unto God a more excellent sacrifice than Cain by which he obtained witness that he was righteous, God testifying of his gifts" "And the Lord had respect unto Abel and to his offering: but unto Cain and to his offering He had NOT respect" (Genesis 4:4-5).

Clearly, acceptance of the person MUST precede the acceptance of the service; and the acceptance of the person is by faith. Both men offered an excellent sacrifice. The sacrifice of Abel had no more efficacy in itself than the offering of Cain, to commend him to the favor of God.

Abel was not accepted on account of his offering; nor was Cain rejected on account of his. But Abel had faith and a revelation of the original sin, and that he was the true seed of Adam for whom the True Seed of the woman would give His life. He was justified to God by a faith which was expressed in his sacrifice -- an eye for an eye, and a life for a life -- speaking of the coming Kinsman Redeemer.

"Without shedding of blood is no remission" (Hebrews 9:22). For the life is in the blood which is the evidence the life has been sacrificed. The innocent life of the lamb typed Christ, "the Lamb slain from the foundation of the world" (Revelation 13:8) Whose innocent life was given in substitution for the guilty lives of Adam and his seed.

Cain, on the other hand, presented an offering of the first fruits without faith. He actually believed he was Adam's firstborn, and with no revelation of the original sin, understood no need for a substitute life to be offered. (Of course the Lamb, which represented Christ the second Adam, could NOT be applied to Cain who is NOT in Adam's race and has NO substitute). Cain therefore offered the first fruits of the harvest, a type of adoption, placement, or recognition of a son -- the baptism of the Holy Ghost or new birth -- WITHOUT a blood offering, and was REJECTED by God because he was NOT God's Son. Neither was he Adam's son.

Cain was "born in sin:" death stood between him and Jehovah. But in his offering, there was no recognition whatever of this fact. He treated Jehovah as though He were, altogether, such as himself, who could accept the sin-stained first fruit of a cursed earth without the blood atonement.

Cain saw no need for Atonement and in type, sought to be placed as a son (or born-again) without Calvary. Cain was NOT a son of God, he had NO faith (I John 3:4-10). Cain obtained witness that he was UNRIGHTEOUS but went about to establish a righteousness of his own, bringing an offering as one entitled in his own name, to present it, -- as one seeking, by means of it, to satisfy his God. His was not the guiltless simplicity and uprightness of a sinner receiving a free pardon, and in consequence, rendering a free service, forgiven much, and therefore loving much. His was the cold and calculating homage of contented self-confidence, paying, more or less conscientiously, its due to God, with heart unbroken by any true sense of sin, and spirit unsubdued by any melting sighs of the riches of redeeming love.

"Cain was begotten of that wicked one and slew his brother. And wherefore slew he him? Because his own works were EVIL, and his brother's righteous" (I John 3:12). He was not the son of Adam, who was "the son of God" (Luke 3:38). The Bible establishes every Word in the mouth of two or three witnesses. To demonstrate further to future generations of Bible believers that there existed NO relationship between God and Cain, He gave him an opportunity of finding the acceptance Abel had found. By faith. But instead of humbling himself to penitence and faith, God's grace provoked in Cain wrath, and he frowned upon God (Genesis 4:5).

Still God pleaded with him and said, "when you fail, I have provided a sin offering." It was very near him, he did not need to work or strive for it, it was already at his disposal and subject to him; it may be appropriated and used by him and awaits his pleasure. Cain had but to go to the door of Abel's sheepfold, take and offer a lamb by faith -- and he would have been accepted by God and still had Abel's respect as his elder brother. But it must be offered by faith, but when faith was revealed, Cain knew clearly he had NO claims upon God through Christ, OR the birthright.

Now, sin is to Cain as Eve was to Adam -- flesh of his flesh, and Cain is to rule over sin as man is to rule over his wife. The natural mind is the mark of the beast, and the way of Cain {Jude 10-16}. Wisdom versus faith -- creeds and trinities, etc., against the revealed Word of God. The enmity of Cain's carnal mind, his INTELLIGENCE, however, prevailed. Cain could NOT be subject to the Law of God; nor would he submit himself to the righteousness of God. He was enmity with God and enmity with the seed of Adam {Genesis 3:15; Romans 8:7; I John 3:12}.

When Cain's anger could not reach the great Being of whom chiefly he complained, he vent it on his brother who was within his reach, when Abel reluctantly shared the revelation which amply revealed the original sin, showing that Cain was NOT Adam's son, NEVER had the birthright, and is NOT redeemable.

After the murder, Cain deliberately determined not to revisit the sanctuary - "the Presence of the Lord," {for it is afterward said that upon receiving his sentence, he departed thence}, confident he has settled the matter of primogeniture and inheritance by slaying Abel. In his confidence he even assumes an air of defiance, almost as if he were the wronged and injured party.

"WHERE IS ABEL THY BROTHER"?

"I know not," is his impatient and unfeeling reply - "Am I my brother's keeper? {My brother might have kept himself. Or his God with whom he was so great a favorite, might have kept him}" Thus Cain exults in his success, in getting the better of the feeble and unprotected simplicity of his righteous brother, and almost upbraids the Lord with the little care that He seems to take of His own.

But Abel's blood had a voice, for "precious in the sight of the Lord is the death of His saints", and "He makes inquisition for blood" (Genesis 4:10; Psalms 116:15; 8:12). Abel is the first of that noble army of martyrs, "whose righteous blood" would come on the people that rejected the Lord's first Coming (Matthew 23:35), and the spiritual serpent seed, who have rejected Him since, and are today crucifying Him afresh unto themselves and the world {Revelation 5:9-10; 17:6; 18:24}. Cain, on the other hand, is doomed to be a castaway, as are all his seed and those of Adam's race without the faith of Abel.

Cain was so apprehensive of that doom he cried, "It shall come to pass, that every one that finds me shall slay me." So God set a mark on him, {and every religionist has it}, and stated "whosoever kills Cain, vengeance shall be taken sevenfold". But for this express prohibition, the murderer's fear would infallibly and justly, have been realized. The murderer, Lamech, in a subsequent generation, imitating Cain's example, gloried in his impunity {Genesis 5:24}; and soon the earth was filled with violence. As we read and daily witness, the days of the Coming of the Son of man resemble these days immediately before the flood {Matthew 24:37}.

The murderer is once again exempt from the punishment of death and the earth is again filled with violence and lawless infidelity as in the age which the flood surprised. So evil will times become in Daniel's Seventieth Week, that the church will slay the scanty remnant of the woman's seed {foolish virgin}, and those which keep the commandments of God, and have the testimony of Jesus Christ, the 144,000 elect Israelites {Revelation 12:17; 6:11; 14:12-20; 17:6; 18:24}.

One cannot 'give' faith, only 'receive' It. God is the only One Who can 'give' faith. As a Christian brother and minister of God I will share but cannot 'give' my faith to another. God alone is the Giver of faith and every good gift. If we sincerely desire faith in His revealed Word above our necessary meat, we will approach the written Word with prayerful reverence, always prepared to be found wrong, knowing assuredly the whole Bible is inspired and without contradiction.

In summary we have seen Eve was beguiled by the Serpent, then introduced her husband to the mystery of procreation, and was in Genesis 3 already mother of all that is living, bearing in her womb the seed of the Serpent and the seed of Adam. What doctors call 'a case of superfetation'.

God's law of reproduction requires every seed bring forth of its 'own' kind, so there can be no change in specie. God's plan was for man and woman to reproduce life through the marriage union, but from the first conception, the fruit of sexual union has been DEATH and not life. Clearly, the Word of His commandment of Genesis 1;28 which was ordained unto life (John 6:63), was from the beginning perverted to something which was no longer His Word. It was altered as the denominations have added to and diminished His Word to write creeds, becoming anti-Word and antichrist and no longer His Word, and ordained to DEATH (Revelation 22:18-19).

A link between sin, sexual conception and death is evident from the Fall as man is "conceived in sin and shapen in iniquity." "What is man that he should be clean? and he which is born of a woman, that he should be righteous?" "Man that is born of woman is of few days, and full of trouble," and "the wages of sin is death" (Psalms 51:5; Job 15:14; 14:1; Romans 6:23).

Without faith, or a revelation of what took place in the garden of Eden, causing the downfall and degradation of the human race, it must seem indeed strange that birth by woman, which was ordained to bring life, should bring death, whilst birth by the Man, the Word, brings Eternal Life. Clearly our natural birth is NOT by the Word and NOT fulfilling Genesis 1:28 as God intended, but is after SIN.

You surely see that SIN was associated with birth from Eve's FIRST conception - Cain - because it resulted in DEATH, not life, bringing God's curse upon the Serpent, his seed born of woman, and upon the earth {Genesis 3:14-20; I Timothy 2:14-15; I John 3:12}. The curse will remain upon the earth until it is regenerated, the serpent will be eternally on his belly, but the serpent seed is anathema and will be utterly destroyed.

If God opens our eyes of understanding we will surely see that Satan used the serpent as his agent of temptation -- before God changed his form and placed him on his belly. And it was not an apple which caused the Fall or that made the first couple, who had been naked and not ashamed, aware of sexual differences and the purpose of their reproductive organs, feel so shameful that they covered their genitals from one another and from God.

Finally, if Christ was the prophetic seed of the woman born without sex, Cain was the seed of the woman born without human male instrumentality. God put enmity between the sons of Adam and the descendants of Cain, and that enmity is STILL there.

The Cainite race is summed-up in six generations with no indication of worship of the one true God, but a devotion to earthly things apart from God, by the natural ingenuity characterized by the race. When this race intermarried with the sons of Adam, God destroyed the world by the flood. After the Flood they spread throughout the world and God told Moses when he encountered them in the Promised Land, he should annihilate them all down to the babe in arms. Their end is perdition.

By contrast, Adam's lineage is summed-up in seven generations, and in the birth of Seth's son came a revival of prayers and true worship whereby the sons of God were separated from the sons of Cain, and called themselves by His Name. Jesus Christ was born of Adam's race to be the KINSMAN Redeemer for Adam's race, whose end is glory.

This enmity also exists between the spiritual serpent seed, or church carnal, and the Seed of the second

Adam, God's elect, for the son of the bondswoman always persecuted the son of the free. But the son of the bondswoman is cast into outer darkness. The Dragon (or spiritual serpent) seed manifest as Rome and her harlot daughters, will seek to destroy the True Seed of the Woman, but Christ will translate His Bride. Satan's church will persecute and martyr the remnant of Her seed and they who keep the Commandments of God and have the testimony of Jesus Christ, then Christ will cast the natural and spiritual serpent seed into a Lake of Fire.

KNOWING THE SUPREME DEITY, THEY THAT KNOW THEIR GOD.

GOD IS A SPIRIT

The Scripture states that, "God is a Spirit; and they that worship Him, must worship Him in Spirit and in Truth" (John 4:24). In Isaiah 43 and 45, we can read that God the Father said that He alone is God... "And there is no God else beside Me; a just God and a Savior; there is none beside Me."(Isa. 45:21) "Before Me there was no God formed, neither shall there be after Me. I, even I, Am the LORD; and beside Me there is No Savior." (Isa. 43:10-11)

In these scriptures we can clearly see that there is only ONE God, (not two or three as others believe) for in His very First Commandment, Elohim (the Self-Existing One) solemnly said that "Thou shalt have NO other gods before Me..." (Exo. 20:3)

GOD'S THOUGHTS AND ATTRIBUTES:

Way back in eternity, before there ever was a star, a moon, or a galaxy, Elohim has eternal thoughts and attributes that He wanted to express and manifest for His own pleasure and glorification. He hath seen all things from the beginning, for He is infinite and all knowing.

Elohim wanted to be God. The word "God" means "an object of worship". But there was no one that worshiped Him at that time and He then created the angels first, so that He as God is worshiped and is proclaimed as God Almighty.

Elohim wanted to become a Father. Yet how can He be called a "Father" when He Himself has no children then? And so in God's mind He wanted to create sons and daughters unto himself so that He could become their Father. Thus, we know that this plan of God was fulfilled and manifested later on. He created Adam and from him He took Eve. It's a type of the church which was taken from the body of Christ, for the Bible says, "we are flesh of His flesh, and bones of His bones."

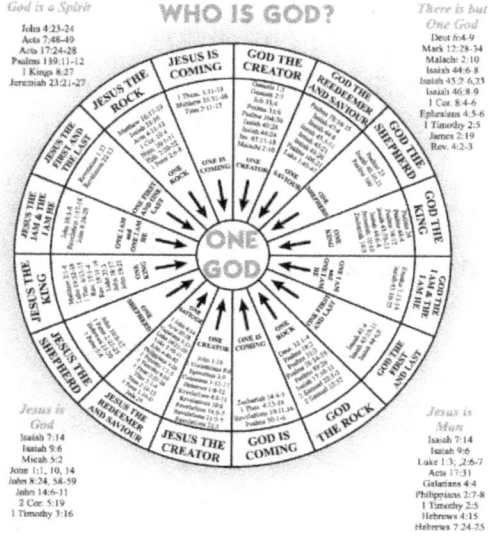

Elohim wanted to become a Savior. But you see, how can He become a Savior when there's no one to be saved in the first place? There has to be a fallen entity first before He could ever display his attributes as a Savior. We can therefore conclude from this case that God hath foreseen the fall of man and He permitted man to fall from grace in order for God to fulfill His majestic plan of saving them. Man was placed as a "free moral agency" to choose for himself between good and evil. Adam and Eve fell for the wrong choice. But God prepared the solution for sin even before the foundation of the world. Revelation 13:8 tells us that the "Lamb was slain "before" the foundation of the world" to act as an atonement for sin. And God wrote our names (God's elected seed) in the Lamb's Book of Life even before man could ever commit sin. Christ came to redeem these predestinated seed.

Elohim wanted to be a Healer, too. Yet how can He become a Healer when there's nobody sick? There has to be a sickness first before He could be a Healer. Which was, the sickness or the Healer? We can then conclude from here that sicknesses and afflictions are part of God's permissive will to man in order to show and manifest to mankind His attributes of being a Healer. Psalms 103:2-3 states, "Bless the LORD, O my soul, and forget not all his benefits: who forgiveth all thine iniquities; who healeth ALL thy diseases." Consider the afflictions of Job, blind Bartimaeous, the woman with the blood issue, and more. They just declared the glory and healing power of God and served as testimonials of God's grace through each generation.

God also wanted to manifest Himself as a King, as a Priest, and as a Judge. So there has to be a kingdom set-up, a holy tabernacle set-up, and a judgment bar set up. These are His eternal thoughts and intentions before the foundation of the world, to get glory unto Himself.

Yet God knew that as a Spirit He will never be able to fulfill these plans of his without having a "body" that will act out His plans. For example, it is written in His Law that "Almost all things are by the Law purged with blood; and without the shedding of blood is no remission" (Hebrews 9:22). Redemption requires death. Can a Spirit bleed and die?

It takes BLOOD, therefore, to pay the penalty for sin. Yet no man's blood, no angel, no priest, no animal's blood, was ever worthy to redeem man in his fallen estate. God must do it Himself, for there is no Savior but Him alone. He must do it in order to show that He alone is the ONLY Redeemer. In Isaiah 45:22, God said, "Look unto Me, and be ye saved, for I AM God, and there is none else." "Thou shalt know no God but Me; for there is NO SAVIOR BESIDE ME". (Hosea 13:4).

God is the only Savior there is. The key to the whole mystery of the Godhead is this. God knew that He, as God, could not die and bleed in the Spirit, for a Spirit has no flesh and bones. His own law required blood for an atonement.

So in order for God to fulfill His plan of redeeming mankind, He had to put on a veil of flesh, in order to taste death and pay the penalty for His own law, to justify the ungodly. That is to fulfill Romans 3:28, "Therefore we conclude that a man is justified by faith without the deeds of the law." "For by grace are ye saved through faith; and that not of yourselves: it is the gift of God: not of works, lest any man should boast" (Eph.2:8,9).

THOUGHTS EXPRESSED INTO "WORD"

God, then began to express Himself from eternity, by His spoken Word. Time began when God started speaking. This great Fountain of Spirit which had no beginning or no end began to express His attributes by the Spoken Word.

Out of the existence of the Father went out the "Logos", which was the Word, which was God's "Theophany". It was a visible body of the great Jehovah God going forth in the beginning. It was called the "Logos", which in the original Greek, means "something spoken; which includes the thoughts of the Speaker".

That Logos was God's "express image". It was God Himself made into Word. That Logos that went out from the great eternal Spirit was called the "Son" of God. It was the only visible form that this Spirit had. And It was a "theophany", which means a celestial body, and that body was like a "man".

Time, then, began when that "Logos" came out of God, as evident in the succeeding scripture. John 1:1-3, "In the beginning was the Word and the Word was with God, and the Word was God. The same was in the beginning with God. All things were made by Him; and without Him was not any thing made that was made".. And the Word was made flesh and dwelt amongst us." (John 1:1-3, 14).

From that "theophany" is where man was also created by God, after His own image, which was a "spirit-man":

> "And God said, Let US make man in our image, after our likeness: and let them have dominion over the fish of the sea, and over the fowl of the air, and over the cattle, and over all the earth, and over every creeping thing that creepeth upon the earth. So God created man in his own image, in the image of God created he him; male and female created he them."

> (Gen 1:26,27).

The "Let US make man in OUR own image" in the above verse refers to God the Father (the Great Spirit) talking, speaking to His Theophany Body, which was His begotten Son. We can see here that man was created from that pattern, with both spirit and body realms. We were never created from the image of angels.

God will speak one of these days, and we'll come forth in His image and in His likeness, men and women, not angels, but men and women. God made Angels; we'll never be Angels. We weren't made for Angels. Men are made men. God made man. He intends him to be man. It's God's pattern."

The "theophany", which was the Son, is also what is spoken of in Col 1:15-17, which reads: "Who is the IMAGE of the invisible God, the Firstborn of every creature: For by Him were all things created, that are in heaven, and that are in earth, visible and invisible, whether they be thrones, or dominions, or principalities, or powers: all things were created by him, and for him: and He is before all things, and by him all things consist."

That theophany of God was then made FLESH on earth later on in the Person of Jesus Christ Jesus through the womb of Mary.

Revelation 3:14 speaks of Jesus as the "Beginning of the Creation of God". That is Who the Lord Jesus says He is. But those words don't mean exactly as they sound to us. Just taking them the way they sound has made some people (in fact multitudes of people) get the idea that Jesus was the first creation of God, making Him lower than Godhead.

Then this first creation created all the rest of the universe and whatsoever it contains. But that is NOT right. You know that doesn't line up with the rest of the Bible. The words are, "He is the BEGINNER or AUTHOR of the creation of God."

Now we know for a surety that Jesus is God, the very God. He is the Creator. John 1:3 "All things were made by Him, and without Him was not anything made that was made." He is the One of Whom it is said, Genesis 1:1 "In the beginning God created the heaven and the earth". Also it says in Exodus 20:11, "For in six days the Lord made heaven and earth, the sea and all that in them is, and rested the seventh day." See, there is no doubt that He is the Creator. He was the Creator of a FINISHED PHYSICAL CREATION.

Surely we can see what these words mean now. To have any other interpretation would mean that God created God. How could God be created when He, Himself, is the Creator?

GOD MANIFESTED IN FLESH

And thus, God fulfilled His plan of salvation, the fulfillment which is written in 1 Timothy 3:16 which states: "And without controversy, great is the mystery of Godliness, God was manifest in the flesh."

When was God manifested in flesh? It was when Jesus Christ was born through a woman; without any resulting sexual act but it was God Himself making both hemoglobin and egg cells in the womb of Mary, God Himself taking the form of a man.

Jesus Christ was the FLESH of God, none other than God Himself creating a BODY of His own. That fleshly BODY was called the "SON", while the SPIRIT indwelling that body was the "FATHER". Not two Gods now, but God veiling Himself in FLESH. That's the reason Jesus said "I and My Father are one." (John 10:30). Philip, the apostle, one time said to Jesus (John 14:8-9), "Lord, shew us the Father, and it sufficeth us." And Jesus answered him saying, " Have I {the Father} been with you so long and yet hast thou not known Me, Philip? He that hath SEEN ME hath seen the Father."

The Name "Jesus" means "Jehovah has become our Savior". Jesus was also called "Emmanuel", meaning, "God WITH us", God dwelling with men.

When the Father decided to come down as our Savior, He put on a robe of flesh and planted Himself, as a seed, in the womb of Mary. This seed was to produce the flesh and blood of the Body He would dwell in as the Son, Jesus Christ. Jesus is God becoming man, to redeem man back to Himself.

God could not die in the Spirit because He's eternal. But He had to put on a MASK and ACT the part of death. He did die, but He couldn't do it in His God form. He had to do it in SON form, as a Son of Man on earth.

JESUS, THE IMAGE OF THE INVISIBLE GOD.

Apostle Paul says this about Jesus in Col 2:9-10: "For in HIM all the FULLNESS of the GODHEAD dwells BODILY, and ye are complete in Him, which is the Head of all principality and power"..."In Whom we have REDEMPTION through His BLOOD, even the forgiveness of sins: Who is the IMAGE of the INVISIBLE GOD... And He is before all things, and by Him all things consists" (Col 1:14,15,17).

JESUS, therefore, is the EXPRESS IMAGE of the unseen God, God creating a FLESH-BODY of His own. And man could have never seen God except through Jesus Christ, the FLESH of God.

THREE DISPENSATION OF THE ONE GOD

"God ABOVE Us" - that's how God was known in the Old Testament, in the Fatherhood dispensation. God dwelling in the heavenlies, where no man could ever touch Him in the 7th dimension.

When the time for the Sonship dispensation came, fulfilling the prophesy of Isaiah 9:6 which says, "For to us a child is born, for to us a SON is given: the government shall be upon His shoulder; and His Name shall be called Wonderful, Counselor, Mighty GOD, and everlasting FATHER, Prince of Peace", these all pertain to the FLESH of God - JESUS, being God Himself becoming Emmanuel, which being interpreted "God WITH us" - God Who can now be touched by the feeling of our infirmities.

It was God also fulfilling Isaiah 53:5, "But He (God) was WOUNDED for our transgressions, He was bruised for our iniquities: the chastisement of our peace was upon Him: and by His stripes we are healed" - all fulfilled and completed at the Cross of Calvary.

In these last days, after Jesus has been resurrected and glorified, God has sent us back His Holy Spirit, the Comforter, to indwell every believer. Thus, we are now living in the HOLY GHOST Dispensation.

As 1Cor. 6:19-20 states, "What? Know ye not that your body is the TEMPLE of the Holy Ghost which is IN YOU, which ye have of God, and ye are not your own? For ye are bought with a price: therefore glorify GOD IN YOUR BODY, and in your spirit which are God's."

THE SPIRIT OF JESUS IN THE CHURCH

JESUS is that self-same Holy Spirit; as He has attested in John 14:18, saying, "I will not leave you comfortless,

"I" (Personal Pronoun) WILL COME TO YOU." "I will be with you, even IN YOU until the end of the world." Gal. 4:6 states this, too, "And because ye are sons, God has sent forth the SPIRIT of His SON into your hearts, crying Abba, Father."

Jesus' own Spirit is now "God IN Us", the "Hope of Glory" (Col 1:27). It is the SELF-SAME GOD all the time, never changing His power, just changed His form from the heavenly to the earthly, and then back again as the Great Spirit, after having fulfilled His great redemptive story.

He was "GOD ABOVE US" in His Fatherhood dispensation; "GOD WITH US" in His Sonship dispensation; and now "GOD IN US" in the Holy Spirit dispensation.

Jesus said, "I AM ALPHA AND OMEGA, the Beginning and the Ending, saith the Lord, Which IS, WHICH WAS, and WHICH IS TO COME, THE ALMIGHTY" (Rev.1:8)

Not three persons in One God, but One Glorious Personage - ONE GOD in three dispensations of manifestation!

JESUS IS BOTH MAN 100%, AND GOD 100%

"LET US" MAKE MAN IN "OUR IMAGE!"

To whom did God say, Let us make man in our image? (Genesis 1:26)

John 1:1-2, "In the beginning was the Word, and the Word was with God, and the Word was God. The same was in the beginning with God."

This Word (Logos) that was with God at the beginning, was the theophany person of Jesus Christ before He was manifested in a physical body at His natural birth.

God is only ONE Person, therefore, in Genesis 1:26, before man was created, God was speaking to the manifested theophany Being of Jesus Christ, even as He later did speak to Christ after He became flesh. John 1:3, "All things were made by Him, and without Him was not anything made that was made." Colossians 1:16-17, **"For by Him were all things created, that are in Heaven, and that are in earth, visible and invisible, whether they be thrones, or dominions, or principalities, or powers: all things were created by Him, and for Him: and He is before all things, and by Him all things consist."**

Jesus Christ, in His theophany form before His natural birth, is the One that created the Angels first, then the universe and all things, and man at last.

And He made the fishes of the sea, the vegetable life. Put the cattles on the hill. It all looked good to Him. Then He said, "LET US MAKE MAN in Our own image, after Our likeness." So He made a man.

God was Spirit; he had to be a spirit man made in His image. He put him here on the earth to lead the animal life and so forth, like the Holy Spirit should be leading the Church today. That was a man. "So He couldn't just leave it in that state; He had to leave something with it. So He said, **"LET US"** (plural) make man (man) in our own image.

LET US MAKE MAN IN OUR OWN IMAGE:

a supernatural being, a spirit man. Yes, indeed. And then when He made man in His own image, he had rule over the beasts. He led the beasts around then like the Holy Spirit's supposed to lead the Church today.

"Now, in this Genesis 1:26, **God made man in His Own image.** But He said, LET US MAKE MAN in our image, after our likeness: and let them have dominion over the fish of the sea,... over the fowls of the air, over the cattle of the earth, and over every creeping thing that creeps upon the earth. **SO GOD CREATED MAN IN HIS OWN IMAGE {singular}, IN THE IMAGE OF GOD CREATED HE him; MALE AND FEMALE CREATED HE them."**

Now here are some salient Biblical truths to notice.

God has revealed tremendous and intriguing things in our day, truths that have been hiding in plain sight all along. Straight from the bible, these revealed truths will strengthen your faith and deepen your understanding of God.

Let's emphasize on this a little more. You'll notice carefully, in Genesis 1:26, God said, "LET US..." Now, "LET US MAKE MAN in our own image." Our," we realize He's talking to someone; He was speaking to another being. "LET US MAKE MAN in our own image after our likeness, and let them have dominion over the cattles of the field." "If you notice in creation, the first thing that was created, of course, was light. You come on down through the creation; the last thing was created was A man.

And the woman was made after man. Last thing that was created of God's creation is mankind. "But when God made His first man, if you noticed, He made him in the likeness of Himself; He was made in the image of God. And what is God? Now, if we can find out what God Is we can find what kind of a man He made."

"And then God taken from his side a piece of him, a rib, and made a woman. Now, where did He get the spirit, woman? See? When He... Genesis 1:26, He said, "LET US MAKE MAN in our own image, after our own--own likeness, created He them man, male and female." He made the burly spirit for the man; He made the tender, little, delicate, feminish spirit for the woman."

That is God unfolding Himself, come the Logos, which was the Son of God or the Word of God. "In the beginning was the Word, and the Word was with God, and the Word was God. And the Word was made flesh and dwelled among us," the Logos. "Now watch, we're seeing God unfold Himself.

And then He put him in five senses to contact his earthly home. He might've given him a foot like a bear and a hand like a monkey. I don't know what He did."

"You don't remember it, neither do I, but we was before the foundation of the world. When God made man said, "LET US MAKE MAN in our own image, LET US give them (plural), LET US get... make man in our Own image (spirit man) and give them dominion over the fishes of the sea, and the cattle's and so forth." Genesis 1, God saying that, "LET US MAKE MAN."

THE LOGOS, WHAT IS IT?

"The Logos that went out of God, form into a body shape. And this body shape was called the Logos, the Logos that went out of God. In other words, a better word for it, was what we call a theophany. (Theophany is a human body that's glorified.) Not exactly with flesh and blood like it will be in its glorified stage, but it is of a form of a human body that doesn't eat, neither does it drink, but it's a body, a body that's waiting for us as soon as we leave this one. Now, in there, we enter into that body. And that's the kind of body that God was, for He said, "LET US MAKE MAN in our own image and in our likeness."

"WAS GOD A MAN? Certainly, yes!

"LET US MAKE MAN in our own image." What was God? A theophany, a body. And there man was made like that and put over the garden. But there was no man to till the soil, in the senses. Then He created man out of the dust of earth, in the animal life, and that man tilled the soil. And the man fell, by transgression. Correctly. And God, the theophany, come down and was made flesh and dwelt among us, to redeem the man."

"Well, my dear sainted brother, my dear sainted sister, before the foundation of the world, when God created you in His image, or created the man in His image, and created the woman in the image of the man for the glory of the man, He made you a theophany just like Himself, when He said, "LET US" to the creatures that He had made, "LET US MAKE MAN in our own image, in our likeness..." a theophany.

God had never become flesh yet; He was in a theophany.

"And Moses saw Him and cried out, "Lord, let me see You." "He said, "Go yonder and hide in the rock, in the cleft. And Moses got back in that cleft; and when God passed by, the lightning and thunders. And as God passed by, He had His back turned. And Moses said It was the back of a Man. Hallelujah.

"Who was It? That's Melchisedec that come down, the King of Salem, with no father and mother, no beginning of days or ending of life. That's Him. And He come down; that's the One that talked to Abraham; that gathered Him up a little body of flesh like that, and breathed into it, stepped into it, and come down and eat a calf, drank milk from a cow, and eat some butter and corn bread."

Now man was the last thing God created. And the woman was made after the man.

Of course, we do agree the last thing that was created, of God's creation, is the mankind.

Genesis 1:26, and God said, Let Us make man in Our image, after Our likeness: and let them have dominion over the fish of the sea, and over the fowl of the air, and over the cattle, and over all the earth, and over every creeping thing that creepeth upon the earth.

Genesis 2:5-7: And every plant of the field before it was in the earth, and every herb of the field before it grew for the LORD God had not caused it to rain upon the earth, and THERE WAS NOT A MAN TO TILL THE GROUND. {notice, the man already formed in Genesis 1:26 was not found in Genesis 2:5 because that he was a spirit man}

And the LORD God formed man of the dust of the ground, and breathed into his nostrils the breath of life; and man became a living soul. Man was first created in spirit form, a spirit man. According to John 4:24, God is the Spirit, and when he created man in His image, He made a Spirit man. See? When we shall see Him we shall be like him. Hallelujah, amen.

THEREFORE man truly EVOLVED from God and nothing else! Ye are God! We came from God, man evolved from God and going back to God our Maker.

THE MISSING LINK IN BETWEEN MAN:

Genesis 3:1, "Now the serpent was more subtle than any beast of the field which the Lord God had made." THIS BEAST WAS SO CLOSE TO A HUMAN BEING (and yet was pure animal) THAT HE COULD REASON AND TALK. HE WAS AN UPRIGHT WALKING CREATURE AND WAS SOMEWHAT IN BETWEEN A CHIMPANZEE AND A MAN, BUT CLOSER TO A MAN. HE WAS SO CLOSE TO BEING HUMAN THAT HIS SEED, DID MINGLED WITH THAT OF THE WOMAN AND CAUSED HER TO CONCEIVE.

WHEN THIS HAPPENED, GOD CURSED THE SERPENT AND THE CURSE MADE IT CRAWL WITH THE BELLY FROM WALKING UPRIGHT.

GOD CHANGED EVERY BONE IN THE SERPENT'S BODY SO THAT IT HAD TO CRAWL LIKE A SNAKE. SCIENCE CAN TRY ALL IT WANTS TO, AND IT WON'T FIND THE MISSING LINK.

GOD SAW TO THAT. MAN IS SMART AND HE CAN SEE AN ASSOCIATION OF MAN WITH ANIMAL AND HE TRIES TO PROVE IT OUT OF EVOLUTION. THERE ISN'T ANY EVOLUTION. BUT MAN AND ANIMAL DID MINGLED. THAT'S ONE OF THE MYSTERIES OF GOD THAT HAS REMAINED HIDDEN, BUT HERE IT IS REVEALED.

IT HAPPENED RIGHT BACK THERE IN THE MIDST OF EDEN WHEN EVE TURNED AWAY FROM LIFE TO ACCEPT DEATH.

Notice what God said to them in the garden. Genesis 3:15, "And I will put enmity between thee and the woman, and between thy seed and her Seed, It shall bruise thy head, and thou shalt bruise His heel." If we give credit to the Word that the woman did have a Seed, then the serpent must have surely had a seed also. If the Seed of the woman was a man-child apart from the man, then the seed of the serpent will have to be in the same pattern, and that is another male must be born apart from human male instrumentality.

There is no student who does not know that the Seed of the woman was the Christ Who came by the instrumentality of God, apart from human intercourse.

It is also just as well known that the predicted bruising of the serpent's head was in actuality a prophecy concerning what Christ would accomplish against Satan at the cross.

There at the cross Christ would bruise the head of the Satan, while Satan would bruise the heel of the Lord.

And here is where and why God made provisions for the Salvation and Redemption of man Jesus, talking to the Jews one day, said, "Your father Abraham rejoiced to see my day: and he was glad." Then said the Jews unto Him, 'thou art not yet fifty years old and hast thou seen Abraham?' Jesus said unto them, "Verily, verily, I say unto you, before Abraham was, I AM" (John 8:56-58).

Who was the great "I AM"? Remember the burning fire that talked with Moses on the holy mountain? That was the "I AM", the self-same Jesus speaking to the Jews. They could not see that Jesus was their own God VEILED IN FLESH.

"The Jews answered him saying, "For a good work we stone thee not; but for blasphemy; and because that Thou, being man, makest Thyself God" (John 10:33). They really failed to see that He was the Emmanuel - both MAN and GOD. Jesus also is the WORD that became FLESH and dwelt amongst us (John 1:1,14).

JESUS certainly was a man weeping at the grave of Lazarus. But when He shouted, "Lazarus, come forth!", and a dead man, four days and stinking, arose and lived again - that was more than a MAN! Who can raise the dead but God alone.

He was a man hungry that night looking on a tree for something to eat. But when He took five bread and two fishes and feed five thousand - that was more than a man. That was the creator, JEHOVAH!

He was a man lying on the ship that night, tired and asleep, while the waves come up. But once he arose and rebuked the winds and the waves and said, "Peace be still!". That was more than a man.

That was God Who can control all nature.

He was a man crying for mercy at the cross, "My God, My God, why hast Thou forsaken Me?" But on Easter morning, when He broke the seals of death, Hell and Grave, and rose up again and said, "I AM HE that was dead, and behold, I AM ALIVE FOREVERMORE!" Who was that? That was the same God Who also said, "I have power to lay my life down, and raise it up again" (John 10:18).

JESUS, BACK TO A "PILLAR OF FIRE"

Let us remember that after Jesus' death, burial and resurrection, Jesus ascended up into the heavens. And when SAUL of Tarsus was on His road to Damascus to persecute the Christians (Read Acts 9:1-5), a BIG LIGHT, a PILLAR of FIRE struck him, and he asked, "LORD, who are You?" SAUL knew that It was the same Pillar of FIRE that appeared to Moses, but that Pillar of FIRE answered him, saying, "I AM JESUS, whom thou persecutest." See, He had TURNED BACK, exactly back to THE SAME FORM before He took on a tabernacle of FLESH - the Pillar of FIRE that met Moses in the wilderness.

Remember, It was the SAME Pillar of Fire that came to PETER that night and loosed him out of the prison cell (Read Acts 12:5-7).

That SAME Pillar of Fire (Cloven Tongues of Fire) appeared on the Day of PENTECOST and set on each of those at the upper room, dividing Himself, giving part of His Spirit among His church (Acts 2).

Peter declared in Acts 2:36, "Let all the house of Israel know assuredly that God hath made that SAME JESUS, whom ye have crucified, BOTH LORD AND CHRIST". There He is - LORD (Fatherhood), JESUS (Sonship), CHRIST (Anointed Holy Ghost) - The LORD JESUS CHRIST, the complete manifestation of the ONE TRUE GOD.

Finally, consider this: Who was the FATHER of Jesus? Matthew 1:18 says, "She (Mary) was found with child of the HOLY GHOST." But Jesus Himself claimed that GOD was His FATHER. Therefore, God the Father, and God the Holy Ghost, make the Father and the Spirit ONE, OR ELSE JESUS HAD TWO FATHERS. But notice also that Jesus said that "I and My FATHER ARE ONE", NOT TWO. That makes ONE GOD, NOT THREE.

WHERE IS PARADISE, HEAVEN AND HELL!

Please read on!!
It's quite intriguing, incisive and revealing
Let us analyze this, by starting with Luke 23:42-43

"And he said unto Jesus, Lord, remember me when thou comest into thy kingdom. And Jesus said unto him, Verily I say unto thee, Today shalt thou be with me in paradise."

This is where we have a new word, Paradise.

Now many times when we hear this word we want to think of it as some place in heaven or according to some, heaven itself. But I am afraid that is not correct!

Now, there was a time that the people didn't go into the Presence of God when they died: the justified. That was in the Old Testament. They went into a place called Paradise, and in there, the souls of the Just waited in Paradise. BUT PARADISE WAS A PLACE WHERE GOD KEPT THE SOULS LIKE A DREAMLAND, UNTIL THE BLOOD OF JESUS CHRIST WAS SHED; for the blood of bulls and goats would not take away sin; it only covered up sin. But Jesus' Blood alone takes away or bleaches sin.

You notice that when Jesus died at Calvary; while returning, He brought out from the grave those dead saints that had died under the atonement of blood of bulls, and goats, and heifers. And they entered into the city (Oh.) and appeared to many.

That is Paradise.

Now we all know that when Jesus died he did not go straight to heaven because according to 1Peter 3:18-20, he went & preached to souls that were in prison.

But one might say wait a minute, in verse 43 of Luke 23, He has an appointment with this thief in Paradise, "... today you shall be with me in Paradise"

True. He had & He kept it. Let me say that Paradise was in the same realm where Jesus went to when he died, - the 5th Dimension.

So Jesus never wasted His time with souls that were in prison. He did a short quick work, they were not going to repent anyway. Then he proceeded to the devil and took the keys of death and hell & was back in time for his appointment with the thief in Paradise because He always keeps his appointments.

You may ask, where do you get that from? In Luke 16:26

"26 And beside all this, between us and you there is a great gulf fixed: so that they which would pass from hence to you cannot; neither can they pass to us, that would come from thence."

So now I hope we agree that this great gulf divided the 5th Dimension into two, separating the regions of the lost from Paradise.

This is the story of Lazarus & the rich man, I am sure you are aware of it.

Though he was in hell, the rich man could still see & communicate with people in Paradise, verse 23;

"And in hell he lift up his eyes, being in torments, and seeth Abraham afar off, and Lazarus in his bosom." Though they could talk to each other, though they could see each other, there was a great gulf preventing those on one side of the chasm to crossover to the other. PARADISE WAS "TAKEN AWAY" or "EMPTIED OUT".

It was that division of Hades or Sheol occupied by elect souls pending the resurrection. It was separated from the souls of sinners in the deepest parts of Hades who had to look up in order to discover the condition of the blessed, for the gulf of predestination was irrevocably fixed between them according to God's foreknowledge of their lifetime decisions freely made. These suffer in torments of anguish waiting the great day of God's judgment.

Both realms are described in Luke 16:19-31.

When Lazarus died and his burial was too unimportant to mention; while "the rich man died and was buried." His carcass was carried in pomp to its earthly resting-place while Lazarus' soul was carried in theophany into Abraham's bosom, signifying that he was elect and heir to the blessing of Abraham. And when the rich man in torments on his side of the gulf lifted his eyes, he saw Lazarus as it were reclining next to Abraham at the heavenly feast.

The rich man knew Abraham and recognized him as his ancestor, and although Abraham addresses him as one of his sons, his natural relationship did not avail him anything, "for they are not all Israel, which are of Israel: neither, because they are the seed of Abraham, are they all children" of God (Rom. 9:6-7).

From the day of Pentecost all the born-again children of Adam are "Abraham's seed, and heirs according to the promise." Thus true and Spiritual Israelites are primarily non-Semitic Gentiles (Gal 3:29; 4:26; Psalm 87:5; Zech 8:23).

The word 'paradise' is absent from the language of the epistles and occurs only in passages that are apocalyptic, and therefore it is almost necessarily symbolic there as it is when signified in the Old Testament by words such as garden.

After the resurrection of the Lord Jesus Christ, when a true believing Christian dies he goes to the sixth dimension -Heaven.

THERE ARE SEVEN DIMENSIONS!

And Paul said in 2Cor 12 that he was taken up to Paradise or the third heaven. The Book of Revelation speaks of "paradise" again.

Now my question is: Is the sixth dimension the same as paradise, third heaven, or what is the explanation for this?

Man lives in a multi-dimensional environment. Heaven and hell is just across the chasm. When we die, we just change dimensions. If you are a Christian and have been born again, you go straight to the Sixth dimension - Heaven

If you are a sinner who missed to heed and/or has rejected the Gospel and then you died without having been able to repent of your sins nor having been able to receive Jesus Christ as your Lord and Savior, you go to a place called Fifth Dimension. Now, the fifth dimension is where the sinner, the unbeliever dies and goes to. The fifth dimension is the horrible tormenting dimension -Hell

1. LIGHT IS THE FIRST DIMENSION:

The first dimension is Light. Without light, there would be no living things on earth. Without light coming from the sun, the earth and everything on it will freeze and will cease to exist. God said in the beginning, "Let there be Light! And there was Light". God Himself is Light. I John 1:5 states, "This then is the message which we have heard of him, and declare unto you, that God is light, and in him is no darkness at all."

2. TIME - THE SECOND DIMENSION:

The second dimension is Time. Time began and was issued in the economy of mankind when man fell from grace. Adam was supposed to be eternal. He was a perfect man created in the image of God not prone to death nor sickness. But due to the Fall, when Eve was deceived by the serpent into eating and partaking with the forbidden fruit and dragged her husband Adam into it, death entered into human life. "But of the fruit of the tree in the midst of the Garden, thou shalt not eat, for the moment that you eat thereof, that day you'll DIE", Genesis 3 tells us. Man began to age and to weaken after the fall. "Man that is born of a woman is of few days, and full of trouble," Job 14:1.

Time will cease one day after everything has been restored by God back to its original condition. The whole nature today is groaning for the manifestation of the sons of God. All of nature has been perverted, and one day, the new Garden of Eden will be restored back by the second Adam, Jesus Christ, to live in it with His Bride. In Malachi 4 it says, "The righteous shall walk upon the ashes of the wicked". II PETER 3:10-12-" But the day of the Lord will come as a thief in the night; in the which the heavens shall pass away with a great noise, and the elements shall melt with fervent heat, the earth also and the works that are therein shall be burned up. Seeing then that all these things shall be dissolved, what manner of persons ought ye to be in all holy conversation and godliness, looking for and hasting unto the coming of the day of God, wherein the heavens being on fire shall be dissolved, and the elements shall melt with fervent heat?" One needs to have the "Zoe" (Eternal Life) of God in him in order for him to live beyond time element. They need to receive Christ, the Giver.

3. MATTER - THE THIRD DIMENSION

The Third Dimension is Matter. "Matter" is defined as "anything that have mass and occupies space". Everything that we see around us, from botany life to animal life, from land formations to water forms, these are known as "matter". Man is made out of sixteen elements from matter. These sixteen elements are: 1. Calcium 2. Chromium 3.

Copper 4. Iodine 5. Iron 6. Magnesium 7. Manganese 8. Phosphorus 9. Pottasium 10. Selenium 11. Zinc 12. Molybdenium 13. Flouride 14. Oxygen 15. Hydrogen 16. Sulfur. If you lack any one of these elements, you will have a system imbalance. You will feel weak. That's why we need to eat, take some rest, avoid vices, and nourish this "temple" in which the Holy Ghost of God dwells upon.

For man to contact his environment, God gave man five senses: hear, taste, smell, feel and see - in order for him to be able to contact the surrounding material world in which he lives. Faith is the sixth sense that God gave us.

Faith is the "evidence of things that we do not see, hear, fell, smell or taste" (Hebrews 11)- yet these things that we believe upon are true. "Fact" is far more different from Truth. It is a fact that every man that is born on this earth will die. But the truth is, if you are born of the Spirit of 401 402 Message Quick Reference Guide God, you shall no longer die. That's according to Jesus Himself: "He that believeth on Me, though he were dead yet he shall live. Whosoever liveth and believeth in Me, shall never die.

4. SCIENCE - THE FOURTH DIMENSION

The Fourth Dimension is Science. Science involves things that are unseen to the natural eyes but they exist based on natural laws, yet are not quite plain to a common man's understanding. Electricity, for example, cannot be seen. But when one gets to know the law of electricity and apply these laws today, he could run a whole city's machineries, lighting systems, communication systems, and transportation systems. When Thomas Edison discovered the principle of light and came up with the light bulb, he unveiled some hidden mysteries from the fourth dimension. When Albert Einstein learned how to split the atom and introduced the theory of relativity, he broke into the realms of scientific advancement which gave man a basis for future discoveries for both human knowledge and progress. Television, as a product of science, for example, can pick up sights of events from far-flung places and bring them to you through your TV monitors live and in real time. This was only made possible when man discovered and caught the lightwaves and radiowaves from the earth's stratosphere. The same technology works for sattellite systems. Scientific discoveries like the Cathode rays, the x-ray and other applications using laser technology can make a lot of jobs easier now than it was before when science had not yet unveiled that such things are real. Television and electricity, according to Brother Branham, was here already even in the time of Adam, but man was not yet able to harness them. How about today's technology such as the invention of cars, bullet trains, submarines, airplanes, rockets and spaceships? The internet, for example, was only made discovered for human use during the last part of the 20th century and is a fulfillment of Bible prophesy. It was prophesied that in the last days, "knowledge shall increase." Consider the invention of nuclear weapons and atomic bombs that could wipe off a whole nation from the map. These latest discoveries are being taken advantage today by mad scientists who could tamper into God's laboratory to find ways and means to destroy their perceived enemies - his fellow mankind. Brother Branham mentioned that most of the sicknesses of people today are considered as "fourth dimension" diseases, meaning, they are brought about by scientific wastes, pollutants, toxins, hybrid food and by radioactive materials. Science came as a result of man's partaking of the fruit of the Tree of knowledge of good and evil. Science is not a perfect will but a permissive will of God. There's both good and evil in science. The gunpowder can help people hunt for food but it can also kill people. Yes, the car can bring people to different destinations but it can also kill innocent lives if driven by drunk and reckless drivers. One day, science will be done away with in the new civilization that Christ will establish upon this earth. We won't need cars there. We will fly faster than the speed of light just like angels do. You will go through walls, just like Jesus did after His resurrection. You will just speak to nature and it will obey you - say, "tree and mountains, you move right there!" Didn't Jesus promised that "if you have the faith of a mustard seed", that you can move mountains and do all these supernatural things? Adam had that same power before he fell. It will be restored back to us by God comes millennium time and the great hereafter. There will be no wars over there. The lion will sit with the lamb, and the wolf with the lad. Everything will be peaceful once the kingdom of God is restored back on earth.

5. HELL - THE FIFTH DIMENSION

The Fifth Dimension is Hell. It is where the wicked and the unbeliever go after they die. Brother Branham described this place so well in his sermon "Souls in Prison, Nov. 10, 1963. Hell is a dimension and is different from Hades (physical grave) or from the Lake of Fire. "Now, Jesus, after He had finished His ministry, preached to those souls that were unsaveable, that could not ever be saved. Now, the Bible tells us that. He went and preached to the souls that were in prison that repented not. When mercy was given to them, they spurned mercy, and now they're waiting for the judgment."

"For Christ also hath once suffered for sins, the just for the unjust, that he might bring us to God, being put to death in the flesh, but quickened by the Spirit: By which also He went and preached unto the spirits in prison; Which sometime were disobedient, when once the longsuffering of God waited in the days of Noah, while the ark was a preparing, wherein few, that is, eight souls were saved by water." "But after the days of His preaching, His ministry continued, because the last group He preached to the souls that were in hell, that could not be forgiven. I clearly read that from the Bible here from II Peter. See? He went and preached to souls that were in prison (which is hell) locked up until the day of the judgment, because, you see, the judgment isn't now, and there's no burning hell now.

Somebody tells you that a guy's in burning hell now, that's wrong. See? A judge of this earth is just enough to never condemn a man until he's brought to trial. And God will never throw a man into the fiery furnace until first He is condemned by God's Own Law. He rejected mercy, so you see, he first must have a trial, and the trial is the great white throne judgment, but now he's in a place called the prison house. As I saw the vision of both places, have by the grace of God (I say this not to be sacrilegious and if it's wrong, God forgive me), I believe I've been in both places (See?), in both places. And I've seen the redeemed and blessed, and I've seen the lost and where they were at. And that's why I stand as your brother today to warn you to flee from that downward path. Don't you never go that road." ("Say, here is a line like this. And in here there's all mortals. On this side, or that side, men are influenced by one side. This side comes from God. This side comes from the devil.

6. HEAVEN - THE SIXTH DIMENSION

The Sixth dimension is Heaven or Paradise. It is where the Christian goes when he/she dies. His/her body lies in the grave, but the spirit goes to a place called "paradise" waiting for the time that Jesus will raise the dead in Christ as spoken in 1 Thessalonians 4:1627. Brother Branham had gone to this place in a trance. Let's hear him explain it fully well (taken from the Sermon "Having Conferences" June 8, 1960: "Now, remember friends, here lays my Bible. If I'm a fanatic, I don't know it. My... If I am, I—I don't know nothing about it. I—I believe my heart's with God, and I believe He's proved that before you. I may be wrong in some things, but if it is, it's—it's unconsciously wrong. See? And then, when we were... I was thinking about that, and I kept hearing something say, "Press on." I said, "Who is that?" I said, "It must be my wife." I said, "What did you say, honey?" She never moved. I shook her. I said, "Meda?" She said, "Uh?" She was sleeping well. And I said, "Well, it wasn't her." I listened again. It said, "Keep pressing on." Now, I know visions. This could have been a vision; if it was, I never had one like it. And I said, "Maybe it's me saying it.".... And I heard it say, "Keep pressing on, pressing on." I said, "Who are You that's talking to me? Who is in this room?" And that's the way it comes, just like visions here. It's just as real, just a voice, just the same as you hear mine, said, "Keep pressing on." And I said, "Keep pressing on?" Said, "The great reward is just ahead." And I said, "You mean I passed the curtain?" Said, "Yes." Said, "Would you like to see it?" I said, "I would. It would help me, if I could just see." And something happened; I felt myself leaving this body. Now, I never had a vision like that. I, looking back, seeing myself laying there, leaning up against the headboard of the bed with my hands up like this. See? And I looked at myself, and I thought, "I'm dying." And I started moving out, and the first thing you know, I—I come into a little place that kindy set something like that. And as soon as I got there, here come thousands of people, and everybody looked young. Now, I'm in a mixed multitude. I'm your brother. And you watch, I say this in the Name of the Lord. You'll each meet me there if you'll be right. But these young girls coming to me, throwing their arm around me and hollering, "My precious brother..." Now look, I've... When I was a sinner, I never run around. I wasn't ornery to run around with women. And I don't care how saintly a man tries to live and how godly he lives, if a woman puts her arms around a man, it's a human sensation. Now, you just might as well... I don't care, you can call yourself sanctified (and I believe in sanctification too), but you're still a human. Just exactly right. And there's a sensation. I don't say you'd do wrong, certainly not. The power of God keeps you, and you go on. But even in that place,

7. GOD - THE SEVENTH DIMENSION

The Seventh Dimension is where God is. God dwells in the seventh dimension. He alone rules the universe by His power and majesty. Heaven is His throne and earth is His footstool. One day, His kingdom will come down on earth. Heaven and earth will embrace together. The power of God will fill the earth and everything will get back to eternity. All those with "eternal life' in them will enjoy the rest of their lives in His presence. Read the whole chapter of REVELATION 21 where seventh dimension coming down to earth is discussed. 1 "And I saw a new heaven and a new earth: for the first heaven and the first earth were passed away; and there was no more sea. 2 And I John saw the holy city, new Jerusalem, coming down from God out of heaven, prepared as a bride adorned for her husband. 3 And I heard a great voice out of heaven saying, Behold, the tabernacle of God [is] with men, and he will dwell with them, and they shall be his people, and God himself shall be with them, [and be] their God. 4 And God shall wipe away all tears from their eyes; and there shall be no more death, neither sorrow, nor crying, neither shall there be any more pain: for the former things are passed away. 10 And he carried me away in the spirit to a great and high mountain, and shewed me that great city, the holy Jerusalem, descending out of heaven from God 22 And I saw no temple therein: for the Lord God Almighty and the Lamb are the temple of it. 23 And the city had no need of the sun, neither of the moon, to shine in it: for the glory of God did lighten it, and the Lamb is the light thereof. 24 And the nations of them which are saved shall walk in the light of it: and the kings of the earth do bring their glory and honor into it. 25 And the gates of it shall not be shut at all by day: for there shall be no night there. 26 And they shall bring the glory and honor of the nations into it. 27 And there shall in no wise enter into it anything that defileth, neither {whatsoever} worketh abomination, or maketh a lie: but they which are written in the Lamb's Book of life."

EXCERPTS FROM GOD'S PROPHET MESSENGER, WILLIAM BRANHAM.

IF YOU ARE SAVED, YOU ARE SAVED!

Now, if you're saved, you're saved. If God saves you tonight, knowing He's going to lose you ten years from today, He is defeating His Own purpose; the Infinite, Almighty, Eternal, Everlasting Wisdom, God, doesn't know enough then to know whether you will hold out or whether you won't? Then, when He saves you, and say, "Well, I'll give him a trial, and see what he'll do," then He does not know the end from the beginning. God knows what He's doing, don't you never worry about that. It's you and I stumbling along. God knows what He's doing. And He knew we...whether we'd hold out, or what we would do.

Now, the Bible said that, Esau and Jacob, before either child was born, God said, "I love one, and hate the other one," before they even breathed their first breath, that His election might stand true.

WE WERE ALL BORN IN SIN!

We're all born in sin. We could not save ourselves. We could no more save ourself, than we could take our boot straps and lift ourself over the moon. We could not do it. We're totally helpless. And therefore, God would not condemn you on those basis because you are a sinner.

He'd condemn you because you refuse to take the way of escape.

Therefore, it isn't God; it's yourself. You condemn yourself. And when you condemn yourself, there's nobody to pity but yourself. That's all. You must pity yourself, because you haven't accepted God's provided way of escape.

Now, when God makes His ways, just wonder how He feels when He makes a way for us, for our healing, for our salvation, for our comfort, for our peace, and all these things, and we just walk away and leave them. It must make Him feel terribly bad.

Isn't it beautiful when you can really anchor your soul into Christ, in such a place till you can get quiet before Him? And hear His Voice speaking to you, saying "I am the Lord that healeth thee. I am the Lord that giveth thee Eternal Life. I love thee. I knew thee before the foundation of the world. I put thy name upon the Book, thou art Mine. Fear not, it's Me. Don't be afraid, I'm with you." Then I sing:

I have anchored my soul in a haven of rest,

I'll sail the wild seas no more;

The tempest may sweep o'er the wild, stormy deep;

But in Jesus I'm safe evermore.

Remember, the very Voice that speaks sweet to you, will condemn the sinner. The very flood that saved Noah, destroyed the sinner.

See what I mean?

REPENT NOW, AND BELIEVE THE GOSPEL:

> *"Then Peter said unto them, Repent, and be baptized every one of y you in the name of Jesus Christ for the remission of sins, and ye shall receive the gift of the Holy Ghost".*

> *Acts. 2:38.*

F or if there is no repentance, then judgment is sure to come!

Hezekiah repented. See? Nineveh repented. But Ahab never repented. Nebuchadnezzar never repented. The people in Noah's time never repented, and the judgment swept right on them. See? Now, He first warns everybody. Everybody gets a warning. Repent or you perish. Lk 13:3-5

Now, seeing the time is at hand, let everyone that feels that there is a warning, repent quickly before the wrath of God strikes.

Now all through the ages and from John the Baptist and all the apostles each one preached and based their messages on repentance for the forgiveness of sin and expressed by bearing active fruit in one's life. Repentance has been the message to the people drawing sinners back to God beginning from John the Baptist, Jesus Christ, and the rest of the disciples; and not the glare that we see everywhere today.

Because by nature, we come into this world through sexual desire, of man and woman producing an earthly child.

And without teaching the child right, he will go the wrong way of life being that it is his nature to do such and is hell bound, if he grows up without repentance. To repent doesn't necessarily mean to try to stop sinning. It can mean a change of mind set, and fearing the Lord. We have two natures after we're saved. Our flesh will still sin, but our spirit is perfectly sanctified. Paul struggled with this as every saved person will.

But when you are repented and born again, then the Light of God shines down into your soul (Amen); then it is no more a dark valley, but a valley with a shadow in it. You may be veiled here in the body with the flesh, and with things known by faith, but there is enough Light in there. You who were once dead in sin has He quickened to life by Jesus Christ. Repent therefore now and believe the gospel! True repentance will bring godly sorrow making us to turn away from our wrong doings.

What is "Sin" that we have to repent from? Sin Is UNBELIEF from what God has said. Unbelief is such a horrible thing, repent or turn away from your unbelief of what God has said, and live right!

In the Garden of Eden the very first original sin was because Eve doubted the Word of God, and we notice that when Satan tempted Jesus, he also tried to use the same technique he used on Eve. Satan made Eve to doubt or disbelieve the word of God and so caused mankind to come short of the glory of God. Let me show you just by the Word.

The first time that the devil met Jesus Christ, he came to make him doubt or disbelieve the word. Said to him "if you are the Son of God..." Doubt always is of the devil. That is where the first sin comes from. There is no other sin but doubt. Unbelief is the original and only sin. *All our wrong doings such as smoking, drunkenness, telling lies, fornication, adultery, idolatry, hatred, murder etc. are just the attributes of* "unbelief". We commit those things because we do not believe.

Absolutely, committing adultery, smoking cigarettes, filthy living, getting drunk or all unrighteousness are attributes of unbelief.

The great majority of people are often confused as to what sins they are to repent from; and because the sin attributes are so many, people grope in the dark getting tossed to and fro their salvation. Again Sickness is an attribute of sin. Sin brought sickness! It may not be your own sin, but the sin of your parents.

But when Jesus died for Sin, He died for every attributes that sin ever produced. So when sin was finished, it was the complete plan of redemption.

In other words, your repentance means that, from the moment you decide to change from your wrong doings, you are saying,

"Lord, enough of following my thoughts, or what anyone else says, but now I want to follow ONLY what you say. I am repenting or turning away from my unbelief and rebellion

against your Word and now have decided to do your will through faith in God's word."

And now also the axe is laid unto the root of the trees: therefore every tree which bringeth not forth good fruit is hewn down, and cast into the fire. Matt. 3:10. For godly sorrow worketh repentance to salvation not to be repented of: but the sorrow of the world worketh death. 2 Cor. 7:10.

How dare anyone claim repentance and continues to live like the rest of the world, or the same way he once lived in the past?

You have to do this, with all seriousness; you have to show forth that you mean it and committing yourself forthwith to live by His Word. And as soon as you genuinely repent and accept the finished work of our Lord Jesus for the atonement of sin, you should without delay immediately, go for immersion baptism in the Name of The Lord Jesus Christ, as the Holy Ghost revealed Matt.28:19 to the apostles. Acts. 2:38. And at this moment, if you are sincere, God is obligated to give you His gift, of the Holy Ghost.

Once this is done by faith, you have shown forth your obedience and the 'Guide' (the Holy Ghost) will guide you into all truth, leading you all the way to His everlasting Kingdom.

For other foundation can no man lay than that is laid, which is Jesus Christ. 1. Cor. 3:11. And are built upon the foundation of the apostles and prophets, Jesus Christ himself being the Chief Corner Stone. Eph. 2:20.

By faith we repent, believing in our hearts that God hears and forgives us. By faith we are baptized in water, in the Name of the Lord Jesus Christ, testifying before many witnesses that we believe and identify with the death, burial and resurrection of our Lord Jesus. And that if God recognizes our faith to be genuine, from our hearts, He takes the third step and gives us the Holy Ghost, sealing us into His Kingdom. Oh my, praise the Lord for His Grace toward us!

Therefore, recognize that each day as a sinner you are walking close on your way to hell and if you are a lukewarm believer you would better repent now! Verily, verily, I say unto you, He that believeth on me hath everlasting life. Jhn 6:47.

Now we can't lose our salvation after we're saved: All that the Father giveth me shall come to me; and him that cometh to me I will in no wise cast out. For I came down from heaven, not to do mine own will, but the will of him that sent me.

And this is the Father's will which hath sent me, that of all which he hath given me I should lose nothing but should raise it up again at the last day. Jhn 6:37-39. And I give unto them eternal life; and they shall never perish; neither shall any man pluck them out of my hand. John 10:28. Now he which stablisheth us with you in Christ, and hath anointed us, is God; who hath also sealed us, and given the earnest of the Spirit in our hearts. 2 Cori 1:21-22. In whom ye also trusted, after that ye heard the word of truth, the gospel of your salvation: in whom also after that ye believed, ye were sealed with that Holy Spirit of promise, which is the earnest of our inheritance until the redemption of the purchased possession, unto the praise of his glory. (Eph 1:13-14) And grieve not the Holy Spirit of God, whereby ye are sealed unto the day of redemption. (Eph 4:30) These things have I written unto you that believe on the name of the Son of God; that ye may know that ye have eternal life, and that ye may believe on the name of the Son of God. (1 Jhn 5:13) For I am persuaded, that neither death, nor life, nor angels, nor principalities, nor powers, nor things present, nor things to come, nor height, nor depth, nor any other creature, shall be able to separate us from the love of God, which is in Christ Jesus our Lord. (Rom 8:38-39).

GOD'S PLAN FOR MANKIND:

*C*hristianity is not a form of godliness, or a ritual of religion.

Now, in the Garden of Eden, when man realized he had sinned (disbelieved) he tried to make himself a religion, a covering, or a hiding. The word religion means "a covering" {man's way of trying to cover up his evil to reach out to God}. And Adam and Eve sewed fig leaves together and made themselves a cover up to hide from God, and that is religion. And since then, it has been a strain for man trying to do or imagine something by himself to save or cover up himself. That is not Christianity.

But you are saved by grace. By God's foreknowledge, predestination, and foreordination. "God predestinated us in Christ before the foundation of the world". There is quite difference between religion, Christianity, and Salvation.

Christianity is the life of Jesus Christ. But Religion is a covering and Salvation is a birth, a gift of God. It is a finished work and there is not one thing man could do to save himself.

God did it by His grace and made us a way of escape by Jesus Christ. Yes sir! Jesus Christ made us a cover by the atonement of blood His blood, for without the shedding of His blood, there is no remission of sin. Hebrew 9:22. God made a way of escape in the days of Noah and those who believed him were saved from the destruction of their soul.

Likewise, those who disbelieved the Word, or the message of the hour that they lived were destroyed by the flood. There is therefore now no condemnation to them which are in Christ Jesus, who walk not after the flesh, but after the Spirit. For the law of the Spirit of life in Christ Jesus hath made me free from the law of sin and death. For what the law could not do, in that it was weak through the flesh, God sending his own Son in the likeness of sinful flesh, and for sin, condemned sin in the flesh: Rom 8:1-3. Your religion without Christ, or even your Christianity without character is satanic. You better believe it.

For the LORD {the Angel Himself} will pass through to smite the Egyptians; and when He seeth the blood upon the lintel, and on the two side posts, the LORD will pass over the door, and will not suffer the destroyer to come in unto your houses to smite you. Exodus 12:23.

We all got to know that there is life in the blood! It is the life in the blood of Jesus Christ upon the individual worshipper on open display. No hypocrisy or impersonation of Christianity and acting up what you are not and deceiving yourself. When the death angel passes by and sees the life of Jesus Christ, the lived life, he will pass over you. It is not the chemistry of the blood but the lived life as epistle reflecting the character of Christ and that is what makes Christianity different from mere religion.

And we do know that the Spirit will bear record for the Word.

Beloveth, there is still time left for the sinner to be saved as long as our Lord Jesus Christ still sits on the mercy seat making intercession, else you will go straight from your religion or Church to hell.

But what do you see today among many Christians? Women want to look and act like the movie stars. The men want to look and act like the television comedians.

And the preachers also want to make their Churches look like modernistic lodge of some sorts, membership and so forth. Some of these preachers see the possibilities of becoming bishops, archbishops or a general overseer, or some big titles like that. But **God only set some in the Church, first apostles, then prophets, evangelists, pastors and teachers, all for the perfecting of the Church to keep the Church in line with the Word. Amen!**

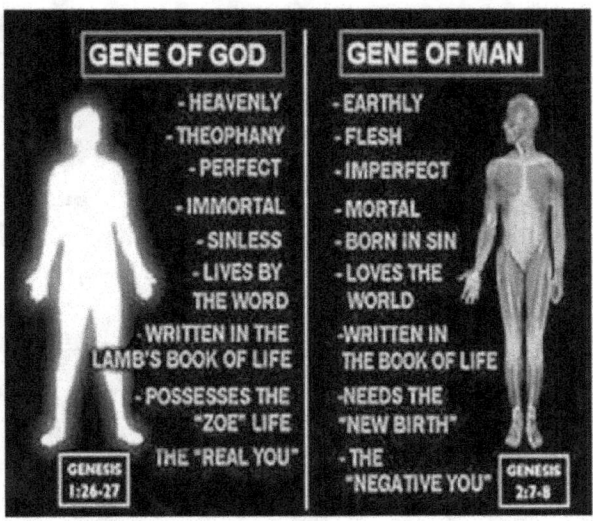

In Gen 1: 26-27 God said, "Let us make MAN in our image, after our likeness: and let THEM have dominion over the fish of the sea, and over the fowls of the air, and over the cattle, and over all the earth, and over every creeping thing that creepeth upon the earth. So God created man in His own image, in the image of God created He, him {singular} male and female created He them.

Notice, He created the Man, male and female, created He them. Now, Adam was both male and female when it comes to being in the spirit of feminine and masculine. And God then took out from the side of Adam a rib and made a woman. But not the spirit, the spirit was part of Adam, for Adam was both man and woman, spiritually speaking, he was created both masculine and feminine.

But in the Spirit or in our theophany, we are sons and daughters, and not some other type of spirit, but a part of the Spirit of the Living God. We are in His likeness, in the perfect image of the Living God, because we are in God's own image and become sons and daughters.

Not separated, but the same Spirit, the same God, the same Person, joined in wedlock to the Eternal God.

And when He separated him {Adam} and put him in the flesh; Gen. 2:18. He just took off the feminine part from the man, and formed the woman as a companion to the Man. And we can say that Eve was not on her own spontaneously created, but a byproduct part of Adam; yes sir, exactly so! She was flesh of his flesh and bone of his bone. Note, let this sink into your heart really good that, that the first "man" was NOT made from the dust. He was in the "image" of God - because God is a Spirit; therefore, the first man was created a spirit-man, but possessing a dual nature. Gen 1:26-27.

Now notice, Solomon by the wisdom of God, was struck by the revelation of his theophany according to

Proverbs 8:22-31. Here Solomon caught this revelation saying, "The Lord **po**ssessed me in the beginning of his way, before his works of old.

I was set up from everlasting, from the beginning, or ever the earth was.

When there were no depths, I was brought forth; when there were no fountains abounding with water. ²⁵ Before the mountains were settled, before the hills was, I brought forth: 26 While as yet he had not made the earth, nor the fields, nor the highest part of the dust of the world"}.

Therefore, if anything is contrary from the normal, then there is a pervasion. When you see a man or woman acting up and being sissified or trying to act like the opposite sex- a man or woman trying to act like man, or a man walking like a woman or a woman dressing up like a man, you know there is something spiritually and fundamentally wrong in that fellow.

Woman be in your place, be subjected to your position as God made you! { thy desire shall be to thy husband, and *he shall rule over thee Gen 3:16b* }.

We are in a perilous time where boys become girls, and women become men and doing that which is uncomely.

Heaven is real, and hell is real! Therefore if you repudiate or reject God's provided way of escape which is in Christ Jesus, you will surely miss heaven, and if Christ is returning right now, you will be in the danger of missing the rapture and of course passing through great tribulation. As it was in the days of Noah, so shall it be in the day when the Son of Man is revealed.

Your miracles, healing, testimonies, or even the substance of riches that you have do not mean you are saved. The rain falls on the just and unjust, and gift and calling are without repentance.

Christianity without Christ is satanic. You speak and sing in tongues, claim to have the Holy Spirit, perform all kinds of signs and wonders, yet disbelieve the Word (the Giver of the gifts) when it is presented to you. If the Holy Spirit indwells in you, why wouldn't you agree with the word and make you say, amen to every Word of God?

Now many people who go to church go for so many negative motives! Some looking for jobs and contracts, others look for wives and husband, breakthrough, just carrying on and following after miracles regardless, but it is only a few out of them that genuinely follow after the Word. Seek ye first the Kingdom of God and His righteousness and all other things will be added unto you.

When Jesus performed miracles, the multitude followed after Him, but when He said except you eat my flesh..., they departed from Him. Why? They want the gifts but never want the Giver of the gifts — the Word. He healed all manner of sickness and disease, and delivered those possessed of demons. They followed Him for what they could receive. Matt4:23-25.

Top of Form Enter ye in at the strait gate: for wide is the gate, and broad is the way, that leadeth to destruction, and many there be which go in thereat: Because strait is the gate, and narrow is the way, which leadeth unto life, and few there be that find it. Matt. 7:13-14.

In our next edition, we shall be writing on "SALVATION BY GRACE THROUGH FAITH".

Because on the Day of Pentecost, we see the Omnipotence spoke and demonstrated Himself. Acts 2:37-38 {It is actually the Acts of the Holy Ghost in the apostles"}. The book of Acts actually shows how the Holy Ghost moved with the apostle. God by His Grace drew all those people together to hear the preaching of the Word that would give them the Faith (revelation) of Salvation; but right now let us devote our energies and times on the subject of WHO IS BORN AGAIN? YE MUST BE BORN AGAIN.

MARVEL NOT, YE MUST BE BORN AGAIN:

According to Jhn 3:7, marvel not that I said unto thee, ye must be BORN AGAIN! And when you are BORN AGAIN, it is not because you believe. They say, you are born when you believe. But the Bible said that the **Devil believes, also.** Now, notice, it is not that, it is an experience.

You say, Well, I have lived a good life. So did the apostles also, but they were not BORN AGAIN until they received the Holy Spirit. They were not even converted until they had received the Holy Spirit. You remember the night, just before the betrayal took place? Jesus said to Simon Peter, when thou art converted, then strengthen thy brethren.

And Peter had followed Him for three and a half years, and had cast out devils, and healed the sick, had preached the Gospel, and still according to the Word was not yet even converted.

No matter how good we are, how much we go to church, or do this, we got to be BORN AGAIN. See? It must be. And God told Adam what he could do and what he could not do. He placed him behind His Word. And then the enemy come in, by deceit, and crawled through the walls of God's Word, cause the door was open to him, and he marred that image, to sin. That's one of the saddest stories."

John 3:3; John 3:7; 1 Peter 1:23.

We cannot easily talk about being BORN AGAIN without saying something about the person of Nicodemus to whom this was spoken at the very beginning.

Now Nicodemus was a Pharisee at the top of his field. Not only is he a member of the Sanhedrin, he was the most renowned Bible teacher of his day, like we also got our modern-day Pharisees of our time. He watched the crowds as they listened to the Lord Jesus, and he knew he has never held the attention of an audience like Jesus does. Jesus spoke in simple terms, but His message has great power. Nicodemus being mesmerized by the life and things Jesus demonstrated, as he observed the miracles that Jesus performed, knowing he has never performed even one miracle. In spite of his achievements, in spite of his prominence in theological education, politics, culture, and religion, yet Nicodemus had a great need. He needed to know God.

The question becomes why did Nicodemus go to Jesus at night? Most likely, he feared that he could lose his reputation as a big time religious leader as we also have our present day Pharisees all over the places today. He may have even wondered if Jesus is actually the Messiah that he had been waiting for whom John the Baptist has heralded His coming. Nicodemus was not too sure of himself! The thing about Jesus having impressed the crowds, irritated the Jewish leaders, and this caught Nicodemus' attention realizing that Jesus taught and acted with greater authority. The basic issue for a Pharisee like Nicodemus was basically on the audacity and authority issue. He probably kept wondering at these.

Therefore Nicodemus made an introductory comment to Jesus, but the Lord Jesus gave it back to him right to the bottom line! Said to him, do you know what? You are on the pathway to Hell, Nicodemus! If you want to get to Heaven, you MUST BE BORN AGAIN. What does it mean to be born again? A Spiritual awakening to the truth of who Jesus Is. We have our physical birth to this earth then, we need to have a Spiritual birth to Heaven. See?

Truly speaking, if you are not Born Again, you will easily be tossed to and fro with any kind of thing that comes, with no understanding. But if your heart is really fixed on Christ and been born again, you will surely understand and believe every Word He said to be the truth. No matter how theologians or anybody tries to explain it away and push it to one side, or to another side. Why? Because the anchor holds!

He promised to be the Same Yesterday, Today, and Forever. Sure, He Is. Then why is He doing it for some and not for others? Now, we are going to know that God is true to His Word regardless.

The reason *you have to be born again* is because you came the wrong way, through the instrumentality of sex. We were supposed to come by the spoken Word. Instead, we come by a sex union between our natural parents, and as the quote above states, our "natural birth" causes us to be born with a sinful nature. Thus, we must be born again by the Word.

And without this New Birth we cannot see {understand} and enter the Kingdom of Heaven.

John chapter 3, and 1Pet 1:23 in the Holy Bible, are very familiar Scriptures to many. And these very scriptures have either been misinterpreted or misunderstood by so many people who claim faith in Christ Jesus. Everyone who goes to any Church denomination claims they are Born Again in such that the very mention of it is regarded as an absolute ridiculous demeaning slogan. WHY has it become so lately?

But this is the Jesus first doctrine -"Ye Must Be Born Again."

Therefore there is something more to that. When you make a step to accept Jesus as your Lord and Savior, by faith you are only believing unto repentance for Justification! You must follow God's process, God's blueprint and God's plan.

JUSTIFICATION BY FAITH, SANCTIFICATION AND BAPTISM OF THE HOLY GHOST.

You are not yet Born Again until you are converted or have the baptism of the Holy Ghost - the Person of Christ living in you burning off all the sin hungers and questions in you. Signs and wonders may follow you and yet you are not born again.

Jesus said to Peter, when you are converted, strengthen your brethren. Peter and the rest of the disciples followed Christ, performed miracles and yet not converted until the upper room experience. "And He said to them, "I saw Satan fall like lightning from heaven. Behold, I give you the authority to trample on serpents and scorpions, and over all the power of the enemy, and nothing shall by any means hurt you.

Nevertheless, do not rejoice in this, that the spirits are subject to you, but rather rejoice because your names are written in heaven." Lk 10:19-20

It makes no difference what anyone tries to tell you. No *man, no matter how smart, what office they occupy apostle, prophet, or titles they claim. He cannot have one thing to do with the Salvation of mankind, because he is a sinner, born in sin, shaped in iniquity, and come to this world speaking lies.*

He is a liar to start with, and any word that he would say would be a lie if it was contrary to God's Word and God's plan.

But God made a plan or blueprint for man to be saved. And man cannot add anything to that plan. It is God's plan. And that is the plan that we want to study in this book. What is God's plan? And He has said, "Let every man's word be a lie, Mine be the Truth." Therefore, we cannot change one word of God to make it something else. No matter how many creeds, rituals, the Church has, we got to forget all about that. This is God's Word. It just can't be done any other way. God made a plan for the Salvation of the souls of mankind.

To be Born Again, you must go through the process of death. Everything does go through this process. You take a grain of corn; if that corn ever expects to live again, it has to die first. If a grain of wheat ever expects to live again, it is totally impossible if it doesn't die first. That corn, that wheat, that flower, that tree, that grass, that vegetable, everything that expects to live again MUST die first. Amen! Jhn.12:24, Rom 6:7-11.

Verily, verily, I say unto you, *except* a *corn* of *wheat fall into the* ground *and die, it abideth alone: but if it die, it bringeth forth much fruit.* If that is so, how then are you going to escape it? You got to die first. You got to die to your pride, die to your human spirit, die to your flesh, die to yourself, die to your arrogance, and die to everything, so that you can be Born Again. You have to do that. If you don't die, you can never live again. You cannot be Born Again if you don't first die. Each day something has to die, so you can live? Oh my, hallelujah amen!

Now, that does not mean to turn a new page as your New Year resolution, but actually die and be born again. Your worldly life will die right there. You have to reckon yourself so guilty in the Presence of God till your worldly life dies right there.

Then the sin question is over for you when you are standing in His Presence. When you look like that, you are sure to live, because you die.

What is the problem with all these people claiming they are born again, when they never died in the first place, without the experience of new birth, without testimony and just carrying on, with the old live? Oh Lord have mercy! The axe is laid unto the root of the tree and every tree that bringeth not forth good fruits is hewed down and cast into the fire.

When He said, "You must be born again," that does not mean jump up-and-down at the altar. That does not mean walk back and forth here and there and shake hands with the pastor or deacon. It does not mean all this foolishness that we have seen being done in some

Churches today. It doesn't mean putting your name on a Church book.

It means death to your first being and live to the second being. It means that the Blood has been applied, and you are identified by the Life of Jesus Christ. And if He is the Vine, and we are the branches, then the Life that is in the branch is also from the Vine. It will bear the fruit from the vine!

And as we can see, there are three stages or sequence of Christian growth, namely:

1. Justification by Faith,
2. Sanctification {cleansing and renewal} and 3. Baptism of the Holy Ghost {the indwelling of the Holy Ghost to guide and empower a believer to live right}.

They are often referred to as the Three Works of Grace. And this is the new birth growth process in the spiritual realm.

To be born of the Spirit is to believe and obey the teaching of the Bible by the Holy Ghost. And a man that's born of the Spirit will obey God's Word regardless of what any tradition tells him. To be born again means to be birthed from above...

THE THREE WORKS OF GRACE:

1. JUSTIFICATION BY FAITH:

Justification is the acceptance and confession of believers as righteous in the sight of God. It is God's acceptance of us for further use. It is just as you pick up an item from the trash with the intention to use it later. By picking it up in its weird condition, is a form of justification. A step of faith, just as if I have not sinned.

Notice when you respond to the alter call in repentance, and accept Jesus as your Lord and Savior, your inner man still almost responds exactly like the world; because you are not yet dead to the world.

You are still alive with all the tastes, and hunger for sin. You know what I am trying to say. All your human hungers or taste to smoke, drink, fornicate, indecent and immoral dressing, fight, anger, dead conscience, and more are still resident within you right there. You know it and that is exactly so!

Sometimes you forget your decision and getting away or out of track in disbelief. And the other time, you are stuck right into it back and forth. Because you are still alive with the human elements of the world! And as long as you are in this life, you are going to have a "carnal nature" that is going to bother you. Certainly as you live in the sixteen human elements, you will surely make mistakes; you will fall; you will willfully do something or take certain decisions that are wrong. And that doesn't really mean you are lost; that means that you are going to get correction for true repentance. What shall we say then? Shall we continue in sin, that grace may abound?

> God forbid! How shall we, that are
> dead to sin, live any longer therein?

> Rom. 6.

Yet by faith you are justified and working out your salvation.

> I am crucified with Christ: nevertheless
> I live; yet not I, but Christ liveth in me:
> and the life which I now live in the flesh
> I live by the faith of the Son of God, who
> loved me, and gave himself for me.

> Gal. 2:20

Even some of us men or women, boys or girls will hardly quit drinking, immoral conversations, smoking firebrands or running around with strange lives, hide and seek. You have never quit lusting after foul women when you see them on the street, instead of turning your back, walking away. Did you notice while you now claimed you have been born again, your old nature still get a hold of you? You still lust right on just the same old way. Why? 1. Pet 1:23. Being born again, not of corruptible seed, but of incorruptible, by the word of God, which liveth and abideth forever. And by this, the old nature is dead, and you got a new nature.

You once were going one way; but now you are going another way. Your affections are set on things above: - a new affection.

> When one be in Christ he is a new
> creature and behold old things are
> passed away.

> 2. Cor. 5:17.

And so is it in the spiritual realm. It is justification by faith, believing on God, receiving Him as your personal Savior is the Justification stage. Now you can see you are not yet born again, but believing unto repentance.

2. SANCTIFICATION:

Sanctification is the process by which God cleanses us from all elements and the desire of the world. {set aside for further use} of whom God cleanses by the word from all elements of the world, and the desire of the world by the word. After you are sanctified or set aside for service, then the Holy Spirit comes in and fills you up with the new Birth as a sanctified vessel.

Cleansing it is a type of sanctification: cleansed and set aside for service." Not in service; for service. Then when you fill it, it is good to go, it is ready for use, and it is finished for service For instance, a glass cup is literally lying out there. You don't just pick it up as justified and set it on your table.

No sir! Firstly, by picking it up is a type of justification. That is how we all came to Christ, that while we were yet sinners Christ died for us. He chose us while we were yet in the pool of sins. Though the glass is dirty, but by you picking it up you are justifying its future usage. And by cleansing it or washing it, is a type of sanctification. Cleansed, and set aside for service/use."

Not in service yet but; for service.

And right after the cleansing, which is herein illustrated as sanctification or set aside for further use: the word of God, cleanses the spirit being from all elements of the world, and the desire of the world. And then the Holy Spirit comes in and gives new Birth and fills up that sanctified vessel. So sanctification is the process by which God cleanses us from all elements and the desire of the world. What do you do with a new baby as soon as he is born? You wash him. And as soon as a man has died to himself and is born of God, he is washed by the water of the Word.

Why then do you dress like the world, act like the world, talk like the world, make friends with the world, be influenced by the world in such that you still live the same way that you were before you claimed to have been born again. Nothing seems to have had changed from your previous way of living. You disregard the word of God 2.Cor. 6:14 " Be ye not unequally yoked together with unbelievers: for what fellowship hath righteousness with unrighteousness, and what communion hath light with darkness?"

By this new birth experience, you are supposed to now fully testify that you are converted; you are born again as you begin to produce the evidence without struggling. Therefore, if any man be in Christ, he is a new creature: old things are passed away; behold all things are become new." 2. Cor 5:17

That man will say whatever the word of God says because God says you are washed by that water of the Word. The cleansing begins by the Word of God! Jhn 17:17. Sanctify them through thy truth: thy word is truth. Eph 5:26. That he might sanctify and cleanse it with the washing of water by the word.

And when that sacrifice has been received, you are dead and that sacrifice is burnt off by fire, and it goes up with your sacrifice into the heaven, and you're sealed away from the things of the world.

You are not converted until you have received the Holy Ghost as evidenced with the disciples on the day of Pentecost.

And here, Jesus speaking to the Father said 'sanctify them through thy truth: thy Word is truth'. Jn. 17:17. He said, "Don't rejoice because the devils are subject unto you but rejoice because your name's in the Book." Notice that Judas was also right there with them while they testified. See how close he came, three works of grace right on up through justification, move right into sanctification, and by foreknowledge, and predestination, he was not converted and did not receive the baptism of the Holy Ghost. So he went into perdition. Jhn. 17:12.

Again, Peter had been saved; he believed on the Lord and followed Him. He gave him power against unclean spirits and sanctified him. And he became the chief spokesman of the apostles, yet Jesus said to him, the night of His betrayal..."Before the cock has crows, you will deny Me three times." I have prayed for you, and after you are converted, then strengthen your brethren.

Notice that Peter had shouted; and had probably danced in the Spirit; and had done all kinds of things but had not received the Baptism of the Holy Ghost yet. And Jesus said to him when you are converted, strengthen your brethren.

3. BAPTISM OF THE HOLY GHOST:

Then when you fill it up, it is a type of being filled with the Holy Spirit and put in service. God breathed breath into the nostrils, spiritually, of Adam, and he became a living soul. Did you know the believer, is born of the breath of God? *And the same way, Jesus breathed on the disciples and said receive ye the spirit. Jhn. 20:22.* it was a promise He gave them; breathed upon them and said, "Receive ye the Holy Ghost." They went to the upper room to wait for the promise to be fulfilled.

The same thing it is when they lay hands upon you to be healed; you may still go on about your business and by faith waiting for the promise to be fulfilled.

But now that I am born again with no denominational Church creeds or dogmas, but entirely on God's solid word alone.

If you are just born by the Church creeds and dogmas, then you have Church fathers, Church mothers. You can call him your father or daddy this or father that" or "your mother this or mama that or whatever they call them today. It is entirely your choice if you want to.

You just call him anything you want to, because he is your "Church spiritual father" or Church spiritual mama or whatever.

They criticize and condemn the mother church and are right back like dogs leaking their vomits. Doing the same thing the mother Church does.

Then how are you calling your Church pastors "daddy, father, and your pastors' wives, mummy, mama and stuffs like that; like the orthodox mother Church call their priests, what did the scripture tell us about this? And call no man your father (spiritual father) upon the earth: for one is your Father, which is in heaven. But ye all are brethren. But be not ye called Rabbi: for one is your Master, even Christ; and all ye are brethren". Matt 23:8-10.

Did I hear you say it does not matter? But who hath bewitched or hinder you that ye should not obey the truth? A little leaven leaveneth the whole lump. Gal 5:9. It is the same Nicolaitan spirit that conquered the laity in the olden Church has crept into the present day Churches.

But if your Father is God, and you are born in the family of God, then you seek those things that pertain to God. Because you are God's child. Your nature is God's nature. Then when you can hear some of them say, our Church believes the days of miracles are passed." That is not true. How could you believe the days of miracles are passed when the very nature of God is in you?

Your new Life in Christ is a miracle. Even your nature is a miracle, how can you look back and say, "The things are dead.

You are a new creature and that on its self is a miracle, new creation. Sure you are absolutely. You better believe it.

And it was on the day of Pentecost that they got experience of the fullness of the Holy Spirit. Then said Jesus to them again, Peace be unto you: as my Father hath sent me, even so send I you. And when he had said this, he breathed on them, and saith unto them, Receive ye the Holy Ghost: Jn 20:21-22.

Things are now different, and something has happened to you. The things you loved doing in the past, you do them no more; you are already a changed person,

Justified by faith, Sanctified by the word, and Baptized by the Holy Ghost.

You are now Born Again with experience.

Being born again, not of corruptible seed, but of incorruptible, by the Word of God, which liveth and abideth forever. 1Pet.1:23. Glorious hallelujah, amen!

Today, many Christians grope in the dark and have been so confused about what the evidence of the Holy Ghost is. Satan can impersonate any kind of a gift, but he cannot take that Word. Try them by the word and they usually fail. Give him the word test, and he will surely repudiate it yet claiming to speak and hear from God.

That is where he failed in the Garden of Eden. That's where he has always failed and that is where the "false, anointed ones" can be anointed with the Spirit, speak in tongues, sing, dance, shout, preach the Gospel, and still a devil.

The Baptism of the Holy Spirit is a definite experience that a person must receive and that is a genuine faith in the promised Word. " **For the promise is unto you, and to your children, and to all that are afar off,** *even* **as many as the Lord our God shall call". Acts 2:39**

The evidence of the Holy Ghost is the fruit of your Spirit.

Jesus said so, "By their fruit ye shall know them." (Matt.7:16-20). "And the fruit of the Spirit is love, joy, peace, long- suffering, goodness, peace, gentleness, meekness (Gal. 5:22).

And the fruit of the enemy is enmity, hatred, malice, strife, and so forth; those are the fruits of the enemy." (Gal. 5:19-21). So, you can judge by the way you are living, if you are standing with God. If your whole heart is in love with Him, and you love Him by keeping His commandments, then you know you have passed from death unto Life (John 5:24).

If it isn't, you are just impersonating being a Christian by which, all carnal impersonations will surely be exposed.

When that soul of yours will line with the Word of God in every respect, it shows you have drawn your life through God's filter that makes you hunger for God (Matt. 5:6).

You cannot receive the Holy Ghost without knowing you have Him. There is something that changes in you. Your whole system, your whole spiritual system is made new again, and you become a new creature in Christ, as the Bible puts it, a new creation in Christ (2 Cor. 5:17; Gal. 6:15).

The same Person in the form of the Holy Spirit, coming upon you as a Token that your life and your fare are paid.

> That you have been accepted. Until
> that Token comes, you are not permitted
> in the bus (Isaiah 35:8-10).

You are not permitted to go in until you can present this Token, and that Token is your fare (Exo.12:13). And now, it shows that the Blood has been shed and been applied to you, the price has been applied to you, and you're accepted.

When I see the blood, I will pass over you. That is when I see the life that is in the blood. It is NOT the chemistry or liquid blood but the very life of Jesus Christ displayed upon the individual worshipper, from inside out. Yea, when I see the blood displayed or applied on the individual worshipper, I will pass over you.

A living epistle read by all men, being the character and life of Jesus Christ in you will be on open display. Now it's not the mental conception of preaching or, if you will pardon my expression, you can call it "talkingfestation", but it is the open manifestation of the true life of Christ, as is read and preached. In Antioch, the disciples demonstrated the life of Jesus Christ and were called Christ-ians. See? Confess it and live the life! When the angel sees the blood, that is the life on display, which is the life of Jesus Christ, lived by, and demonstrated on open show, he will pass over you. Not the liquid chemistry of the blood, or vain repetition of calling the blood of Jesus, the blood of Jesus like that; but the life that is in the blood on display. When I see the life, when I see the blood, I will pass over you. Amen. When you are baptized with the Holy Spirit, you are so in love with Christ and believe every Word that He says to be the Truth.

That is the evidence that you have the Holy Spirit.

And your life is as rest, full of joy; everything becomes different than what it used to be. The sin question is annihilated and you struggle no more with sin. That is the Holy Spirit. That is when you are now truly Born Again and been sealed by the Holy Spirit till the day of your redemption. Oh praise God!

In whom ye also *trusted*, after that ye heard the word of truth, the gospel of your salvation: in whom also after that ye believed, ye were sealed with that Holy Spirit of promise, **which is the earnest of our inheritance until the redemption of the purchased possession, unto the praise of his glory. Eph. 1:13-14.**

As you can now see, Christianity is a lived life. It is not what you pretend to be; you have got to have it. It is something that is real. Christianity is not based upon reformation, reincarnation or as your New Year resolutions, but Christianity is based upon resurrection; the same one that went down is the same one that came back again. It is a proof of the resurrection

It is a sacrificed life, hidden life with God through Christ, and sealed by the Holy Ghost. Character is what God is looking at to find, somebody He can get His hands on, somebody that will stand still long enough. Christianity without character is satanic.

THE THREE DIMENSIONS OF MAN -BODY, SPIRIT AND SOUL.

*N*ow outside of the man is:

1. THE BODY, which is composed of five senses namely - See, Hear, Taste, Smell and Feel. Then inside of the body comes the next -

2. THE SPIRIT, which also has five inlets - memory, conscience, reasoning, imagination and affection. And then the central realm of man is

3. The SOUL, which is also the innermost being of man. The Soul has only two faculties - it is either controlled by Faith or Doubt, or controlled by God or by Satan.

OUTER INFLUENCES
(CARES OF THE WORLD)

Now the Soul controls the Spirit, and the Spirit controls the Body.

Your soul is part of God, and an attribute of God, displayed in a compartment earthly human body. And this body has to be redeemed. But, **the Soul has been redeemed, because it was in sin.** So God came down, by a process of Justification, Sanctification, Baptism of the Holy Ghost, and then redeemed **your S**oul.

The soul is the control center of the spirit. The animal has spirit like man, but has no conscience In fact, it is on record that in the human heart, or in the center of the human heart, is a little compartment where the blood cell never touches. The animal life does not have it, but the human has it. The Soul lives in the heart.

A man believes in his heart. You think with your mind. God stays on the control tower in your heart, controlling your emotions, controls your faith, and controls all you are.

The devil chose man's head for his control tower, and gave him the Tree of Knowledge of Good and Evil. But God chose the man's heart for His control tower and gives him the Tree of Life. The devil makes man see things and looks through his eyes. But God in man's heart makes him believe things that he cannot see. Faith is the evidence of thing not seen. In the heart of man is the throne of God.

1Cor. 3:16-17.

> Know ye not that ye are the temple of God, and that the Spirit of God dwelleth in you? If any man defile the temple of God, him shall God destroy; for the temple of God is holy, which temple ye are.

But sin marred man's Soul. "And after this man sinned, he marred that soul. Darkness comes into it. And then God came down in the flesh OF Jesus to redeem man, but firstly lived with man, suffered with man, and then redeemed man. How did he do that? The Holy Spirit comes into man and drives that blackness and sin away from him, and brings man back into perfect fellowship, as a part of God. By the Blood of Christ, Who cleanses us from sin {unbelief}, we become sons and daughters of God."

Outside of the man is the Body, which is composed of five senses - See, Hear, Taste, Smell and Feel. Then inside of the body comes the next - Spirit, which also has five inlets - memory, conscience, reasoning, imagination and affection.

And then the central realm of man is the Soul, which is also the innermost being of man. What is a soul? It's you! You are a Soul. That Soul has to be changed and be born again.

The Soul is the nature of the Spirit. The Soul has only two faculties - it is either controlled by FAITH or DOUBT and controlled by God or by Satan. Now, the Soul is redeemed, because it was in sin. So God come down, by a process of Justification, Sanctification, Baptism of the Holy Ghost, and redeemed **your soul.**

Rom 3: 23.

For ALL have sinned, and come short
of the glory of God.

1. Jhn 1:8-10 - If we say that we have no sin, we deceive ourselves, and the truth is not in us. If we confess our sins, He is faithful and just to forgive us [our] sins, and to cleanse us from all unrighteousness. If we say that we have not sinned, we make Him a liar, and his Word is not in us. Ezek.

18:4, 21, 26, 27: "Behold, all Souls **are mine; as the Soul of the father, so also the Soul of the S**on is mine: the soul that sinneth, it shall die.

But if the wicked will turn from all his sins that he hath committed, and keep all my statutes, and do that which is lawful and right, he shall surely live, he shall not die.

Again, when the wicked man turneth away from his wickedness that he hath committed, and doeth that which is lawful and right, he shall save his soul alive.

Because he considereth, and turneth away from all his transgressions that he hath committed, he shall surely live, he shall not die."

This is why the NEW BIRTH is required and "Except a man be born again, he cannot enter into the kingdom of God" (John 3:3)

NOW CONSIDER THESE.

Before Adam existed in the flesh, he already had been in Genesis 1:26, And God said, Let us make man in our image, after our likeness: and let them have dominion over the fish of the sea, and over the fowl of the air, and over the cattle...

Now according to John 4:24, God is a SPIRIT, therefore, if God created man in His image, what type of man did He create? God created a spirit man! For that which is born of the Spirit, is Spirit, and that which is born of the flesh, is flesh, John 3:6.

If you would notice, God had already created man in Gen 1:26, now how come that there was no physical man to till the ground in Genesis 2:5?

Adam had not put on the earthly flesh. Gen2:7. The spiritual soul or theophany was the Seed of God. And the LORD God formed man of the dust of the ground and BREATHED INTO HIS NOSTRILS THE BREATH OF LIFE; AND MAN BECAME A LIVING SOUL.

ACCEPTING JESUS AS YOUR LORD AND SAVIOR:

As you boldly step out to accept Jesus as your Lord and Savior, I pray that the Holy Spirit will sink His Word into your heart.

You ought to give the most earnest heed to the things which you have heard and been led to, study the word to show yourself approved and worthy of this vocation and keep on believing the Word.

How are we saved? If you only believe and confess with your mouth the Lord Jesus and believe in your heart that God raised Him from the dead, you will be saved. It is so simple!

By works of faith and now as soon as by faith the sinner man confesses with his mouth the Lord Jesus Christ and believe in your heart that God raised Him from the dead, you will be saved.

You are by this very act justified by faith, as if you never sinned! And faith without works is dead. Now when you confess and have given your life to Christ; you are believing and resting your faith upon His finished works.

And every true genuine gift of God will point to Calvary by the finished works of our Lord Jesus Christ. God has no grandchildren.

God has sons and daughters! Any individual worshipper that comes to Christ must individually come to Him by this same process.

There on Calvary, He paid it all for your sake and by faith you just have to accept the sacrifice made for the atonement of sin.

There is no one can save you; only Jesus there is no one else can add one thing to salvation. It is free if you will believe and just accept Him as your Lord and Savior. Ask Him to come and take control of your live.

Keep on believing and you are saved by the merits of Christ.

Not your own merits; there's nothing you can do to be saved, only believe on His own righteousness. Man has always tried to save himself, and do different things just to be saved by, but by grace are you saved, through faith. Amen.

Congratulations and God bless you on taking the step of faith. After we get saved, we read God's word and start making changes.

The Soul that has undergone the process of the New Birth is under the control of God and will always believe God's Word by faith. And a soul that is unregenerate is under the control of Satan and will always doubt God's Word, and rejecting it in favor of man-made ideas, creeds, philosophies, traditions, dogmas and intellectual conceptions of men.

Ezek. 36:26-27.

> A new heart also will I give you, and a new spirit will I put within you: and I will take away the stony heart out of your flesh, and I will give you an heart of flesh. And I will put my Spirit within you, and cause you to walk in my statutes, and ye shall keep my judgments, and do The NEW BIRTH is the only thing that will produce relationship with God.

Only His sons and daughters are saved, not the members of a church, but sons and daughters. Remember, God has no grandchildren! He has sons and daughters!

Christians, you must have a personal relationship with God in order to be a son of God. He must be your Father, in order for you to be his son or daughter. Exactly so.

God has only one provided way. It is not any certain place of worship Methodist, Baptist, Presbyterian; but it is Jesus Christ, by the NEW BIRTH, believing that Bible. That is God's provided way, and the only way that He has, is in Jesus Christ, His Son. And, in His Son, He placed His Name. God's Name is Jesus, because He came in His Father's Name. You have to be BORN AGAIN to believe the Bible.

FOLLOWING UP OF GROWTH OF THE NEW CONVERT:

The Bible admonishes us that he that wins a soul is Wise! Now we know that newly born babies do not grow automatically. Matt.19:14. And Jesus said suffer little children, and forbid them not, to come unto me: for of such is the kingdom of heaven.

Mark. 10:15.

Verily I say unto you, whosoever shall not receive the kingdom of God as a little child, he shall not enter therein

New or young converts to Christ, have basic developmental needs for their stamina and growth. So you must have the right food formula for the growth of the infant in Christ.

As newborn babes, desire the sincere milk of the word that ye may grow thereby. 1. Pet 2:2. Jesus already admonished Peter and said to him when ye are converted, strengthen thy brethren.

Follow-up is therefore the parental care given to the new converts to bring them up to the spiritual awakening, maturity and fruitfulness. Neglected children usually get sick, and often die or if they live, many of them become delinquent. The same happen in the spiritual realm.

The new convert is gullible and vulnerable to the attacks and ravages of the devil. Be sober; be vigilant; because your adversary the devil as a roaring lion walketh about seeking whom he may devour. 1Pet 5:8. Satan himself is transformed into an angel of light.

> Therefore it is no great thing if his ministers also be transformed as ministers of righteousness whose end shall be according to their works.
>
> 2Cor. 11:14-15.

THE ADMONITION OF OUR FAITH

Someday we are going home. And you are going to chose where you want to be. There is only one way to God, and one way to Heaven. We do not have another alternative way to God. It's

only in Christ Jesus. No one cometh to the father but by me. I am the Way, the Truth and the Door. In Gen 12, we see by sovereign grace, God called Abraham, not because he was better than anyone else, but because God by foreknowledge and election called Abraham; and that is the way He called you. Surely He knows who is going to receive the Word, and who is going to reject it. He knows the end from the beginning.

Notice that God by foreknowledge saw grace in the heart of Abraham and saved him by election and predestination and gave him the promise. "You have not chosen me," said Jesus. "I chose you even before the foundation of the world.

Are you Abraham's seed? Be honest. If God promised divine healing through Christ Jesus, He is obligated to His word.

The Bible said so.

Abraham was called by election, and God gave him the covenant of grace unconditionally. We do know, when God makes a covenant with man, it is man that always breaks his covenant. "By grace are you saved, and not by works, lest any man should boast.

When you come to Christ, everything is settled. "Come unto Me all ye that labor and are heavy laden, and I'll give you rest." It's settled! It's all over. Christ paid the price by His death. The only thing you have to do is to work by faith and Faith is a revelation. Just quit jumping around, getting all disturbed, from place to place, and flip flopping around.

Stand still and see the salvation of the Lord. Only believe all things are possible to them that believe. Amen!

Death is due to every undegenerated soul. Every sinner deserves to go to hell. Every human being should go to hell.

For the soul that sinneth shall die. And all have sinned and come short of the glory of God. After death, is hell: that is what the Word promised.

But love constrained Him that while we were yet sinners, Christ died for our sake. Took our place of sin and went straight to hell and took captivities captive by His shed blood for our sin. You cannot add or take anything away from it. Just acknowledge that you are a sinner, and then accept the sacrifice paid for your atonement by making Him your Lord and Savior.

And remember this; if you lie, or steal, or anything else, God will catch you. Remember, your sins will find you out. It sure will. So, determine in your heart that, tonight, you are going to serve the Lord.

THE TESTIMONY OF EVANGELIST, DANIEL CURRY AT THE GATE OF HEAVEN:

Now Daniel Curry has died and on his way, to the gate of Heaven, he introduced himself to the Caretaker at the gate. And the Caretaker said to him, sir,

"We will look out to see if, you got your name in here." They looked all around; they couldn't find his name. Said, "No, there's no Daniel Curry in here."

"Oh," he said, "surely?" Said, "I am evangelist, Daniel Curry." He said, "I have won souls to Christ." "I have tried to do the thing that is right."

The Caretaker said, "Sir, I am sorry to tell you, there is no Daniel Curry here." Said, "I will tell you what you might do." Said "We have no right here to take your case."

The Caretaker asked him, "Do you want to appeal your case? You can appeal it to the White Throne Judgment, if you want to." But said, "We have no mercy here for you at all, because we don't have you here.

"Do you want to appeal your case?"

Daniel Curry said, "Sir, what more can I do but appeal my case?"

The Caretaker said, "Well then, you can go at the White Throne Judgment to appeal your case there."

Daniel Curry said that on his way, he felt himself going through the space for about an hour. Said he came into a place, it became, and lighter. Said, the farther he went, the lighter it became. It was a hundred times, thousands of times brighter than the sun ever shines. And said he was trembling, trembling. And said, when he got into that Light, he heard a Voice just came out of the Light and asked, "Were you perfect on earth?"

He said, "No, I wasn't perfect," got trembling.

He asked again, "Did you always play honest with everybody?"

Replied, "No." (Said, "A few things came to my mind that I wasn't just exactly honest about.") And I said, "No, I guess I wasn't honest."

Asked again, "Did you tell the truth in every case in your life?"

Replied, "No. I remembered some things I have told that were shady. *I never was truthful exactly.*"

Asked, "Then did you ever take anything that did not belong to you, anything, money, anything else that didn't belong to you?"

Within him, he realized and thought that on earth he was pretty good, but he was condemned.

Said, "No, I have taken things that didn't belong to me."

He said, "No, I wasn't perfect."

{Said he was looking at any minute for the blast to come from that great Light from where the Dove rested,

{"Condemned."}

Said, just then he heard a Voice behind him that was sweeter than any mother's voice he had ever heard. Said he turned to look towards where the voice came from Behold, he saw the sweetest face he had ever seen, sweeter than any mother's face, was standing before him. And said, "Father, Daniel Curry stood for Me down on earth. It is true; he was not perfect, but he stood for Me on earth; Now I am going to stand for him in Heaven. Take all his sins and put them over on My account.

Who is going to stand for you on that day, brother, sister, minister, if you grieve Him away from you today? Surely, if you grieve the Holy Spirit no one will stand for your case when you cross the river of this life.

And if the righteous scarcely be saved, where shall the ungodly and the sinner appear? 1 Pet. 4:18.

Oh, I feel checked right now and can't just go further. Just be fervent, reverently and bow our head in prayers, confessing your sins right now while you pray for forgiveness!

GOD'S CHOSEN PLACE OF WORSHIP:

T he same way you prayerfully choose the wife to marry in good faith, is the same way you should prayerfully choose a place of worship in good conscience of faith. In good faith

here implies that you sincerely desire to seek God to worship and serve God and not with the wrong motives.

You have to diligently and fervently pray real hard to find the God's chosen place of worship so you don't go to any kind of place and worship him in vain according to Mark 7:7. Because any wrong choice will definitely impart to your eternal destination even to your unborn children.

Now if you receive a wrong word, then you will surely receive a wrong spirit. The only right Spirit is the Holy Spirit, and any spirit other than the Holy Spirit is a wrong spirit. 1Pet.1:23 " *born again, not by a corruptible seed, but by an incorruptible seed, by the Word of God which Lives and Abides forever.* " "*Every seed must bring forth after its own nature*", then to receive a wrong Word is to receive a wrong seed, therefore must produce a wrong spirit or a wrong life.

That is the problem with the people with misinterpreted theologies in his dying generation.

For a good tree bringeth not forth corrupt fruit; neither doth a corrupt tree bring forth good fruit. For every tree is known by his own fruit. For of thorns men do not gather figs, nor of a bramble bush gather they grapes. Therefore whatsoever seed **you sow, you will surely reap, literally.** And by their fruits ye shall know them.

Now the only difference between the believer and the unbeliever is that, one heard and responded to what he heard, but the other heard the same Word as well but did not do what he heard. That is God's Law of reproduction. It is the Law of Life. That is the reason we should be careful, and prayerful to choose the right place of worship.

In Deut.16:1-3, we find out that God has only one chosen place of worship where He can meet the individual worshipper.

Thou mayest not sacrifice the Passover within any gate... which the LORD thy God giveth thee:

But at the place which the LORD thy God shall choose to place his name in, there thou shall sacrifice the Passover at evening, and the going down of the sun, at the season that thou comest forth out of Egypt.

And we find out here that He has chosen only one worship place where to meet with His children. "Thou shall sacrifice in the place that the Lord thy God shall choose and they are not to sacrifice anywhere else but in that one place. Any other place would not work. And one place alone is where He meets the worshipper.

God is not a man that He should speak one thing here, and at another time says something different to improve on what He has said.

When God speaks a Word, He can never take it back. He has to ever remain the same. He can never say something, and then say, oh, I didn't exactly mean it. Why? He is Infinite.

He knows the best to begin with.

Therefore He has a provided place, one place alone where He will meet the believing children. And anywhere else won't work.

Remember, Jesus said, when He was here on earth, talking to a bunch of fine people who were very religious, very cultured, a very zealous people of God, but Jesus said to them, "In vain you worship Me," teaching for doctrines, their traditions of men. Remember how pious those people were, and how zealous they were of God?

They were even more zealous than we are today, when it comes to keeping the traditions and laws. And they were very zealous of God, and they believed God.

But Jesus, God made flesh among us, said, "In vain do you worship Me."

He didn't say they didn't worship Him. They were worshipping Him, but in vain. How terrible, how horrible and how disappointing. Oh God please have mercy!

The 2nd verse, says "Worship in the place that I have chosen." Chosen what? In this place showed that He has a place where all people worship. Other places are in vain.

"And in this same place," He said, "I have chosen also to put My Name in this place. I will choose a place, and will put My Name in it.

THERE ARE LOTS MORE DIFFERENCE BETWEEN GOD PUTTING HIS NAME IN A PLACE OF WORSHIP, AND SOMEBODY JUST PUTTING GOD'S NAME TO A PLACE OF WORSHIP. You name it or call the place anything or whatever name you like.

But if God didn't put His name in there, then you worship Him in vain.

But we must find where He chose to put His Name, for it is the place and the only place that He has provided for the Christians to come, and worship Him. What and where would this place of worship be?

And Jesus said in John 5:43, "I come in My Father's Name and you receive Me not," and, there is where God placed His Name, under the sacrifice of His own Son. That is God's only provided Place; there is where people can meet God, That place is in Christ Jesus. That is His provided Place.

There is no denomination, no creed, nothing else that God has promised to meet the individual worshipper. Only in Christ Jesus the only Place His Name is. Hallelujah amen!

But God's Name is the Lord Jesus Christ. That is His Name. He had many titles, but One Name only, "No other Name under heaven given among men, whereby you must be saved." Therefore, we find out God's chosen place of worship is not attached to any certain Church gathering name. It is only attached to where God put His name; the name CHRIST JESUS. There are so many infallible proofs that Jesus is the place. He is the Way, and the only provided Way that God has for man to meet in worship.

I belong to this, and I belong to that." You may belong to that, but till you come into God's provided Place, you cannot get in there unless you become part of that Word.

THE BOOK OF LIFE AND THE LAMB'S BOOK OF LIFE

G od is the Author of Life and in heaven owns a record Book which consists of two parts: one section is called the "Book of Life" and the other section is called the "Lamb's Book of Life".

Now every person that was ever born and will ever be born upon this earth, are all written in the Book of Life: with the exception of the reprobates who are spoken of in Revelation 13:8, *"And all that dwell upon the earth shall worship him* (the beast), *whose names are not written in the Book of Life of the Lamb slain from the foundation of the world. "*

THE BOOK OF LIFE:

A ll whose names are listed in the Book of Life will have to face judgment in the General Resurrection Day and will be judged according to the works that they have done in their body. Hebrews 9:27 says, "And as it is appointed unto men once to die, but after this the judgment. " And Revelation 20:12b also makes it plain -"And the dead were judged out of those things which were written in the books, according to their works". Exactly right!

The names of people who are written in the Book of Life can remain in there or be blotted out depending on their attitude and subjection towards God's laws and statutes.

Generally, this Book of Life is also called the "Book of Deeds" which is our old record, our old union with carnal nature, before we were ever born again by the Spirit of God.

EXODUS 32:33 -

"And the LORD said unto Moses, Whosoever hath sinned against me, him will I blot out of my Book."

REVELATION3:5 -

"He that overcometh, the same shall be clothed in white raiment; and I will NOT BLOT out his NAME OUT of the BOOK of LIFE, but I will confess his NAME before my Father, and before His angels." **Oh** hallelujah, amen!

REVELATION 20:11-15 -

"And I saw a great white throne, and Him that sat on it, from whose face the earth and the heaven fled away: and there was found no place for them.

And I saw the dead, small and great, stand before God; and the books were opened: and another book was opened, which is the Book of Life: and the dead were judged out of those things which were written in the books, according to their works, And the sea gave up the dead which were in it: and death and hell delivered up the dead which were in them: and they were judged every man according to their works. And death and hell were cast into the lake of fire. This is the second death. And whosoever was not found written in the book of life was cast into the lake of fire. Rev. 20:1315. For centuries Churches have thought the concept that after the Great White Throne Judgment all sinners go to a burning Hell and remain there for eternity, experiencing the torments of burning fire.

But is this what the Scriptures actually teach concerning the end of sinners? Let us take another journey through the Scriptures to get a better understanding of **"Hell"** versus the **"Lake of Fire".**

When the Bible speaks of "Hell" and the "Lake of Fire" is it speaking of one and the same place? I can assure you that the Bible is clear in this matter. It is not a "riddle" but a Spiritual "revelation", clearly taught in the Bible. We will be challenged to accept the Word of God or the word of denomination or nondenominational Churches which teach the doctrine of an "eternal" burning "hell" in which humans experience the torment of a fire that does not consume them. To understand what the Bible teaches regarding the end of those judged unworthy to enter into the glories of heaven, Bible teachers and preachers are duty bound to "study the Scriptures" and be honest in what it teaches - staying with the WORD of God and not the Church. We have seen many Church members holding firm to the wrong teachings of their pastors rather than the true word of the Living God.

THE LAMB'S
BOOK OF LIFE:

The "Lamb's Book of Life" is a special section of God's record book.

It contains the names of the elect of God, the chosen ones, the predestinated seed, the Bride of Jesus Christ, as spoken of in Ephesians 1:4-5, *"According as HE hath CHOSEN US* in HIM BEFORE the foundation of the world, that we should be holy and without blame before him in love: Having PREDESTINATED us unto the adoption of children by Jesus Christ to Himself, according to the good pleasure of his will. "

These people are foreknown of God and are redeemed by the Blood of Jesus Christ who was the Lamb of God slain before the foundation of the world (Rev 13:8). Romans 8:30,

"Moreover whom he did predestinate, them he also called: and whom he called, them he also justified: and whom he justified, them he also glorified" (past tense).

Romans 8:33 says- *"Who shall lay anything to the charge of God's elect? It is God that justifieth."* These people were ordained to eternal life and their names can never be blotted out of the Book because they were specially created to be the Queen of Jesus Christ, which is composed of a many-membered Body also known as the Church, the Wife of the King, who is destined to live with Christ in the Millennium and in the new heaven and earth. They were foreknown of God before the foundation of the world as evident in how God addresses his son Job in Job 38:4,7 - *"Where wast thou when I laid the foundations of the earth? Declare, if thou hast* understanding, when the morning stars sang together, and all the sons of God shouted for joy?"

Those that are written in the Lamb's Book of Life will undergo the New Birth in their appointed time on earth.

They will be cleansed, regenerated, forgiven and justified, as 2Corinthians 5:17says,"Therefore if any man be in Christ, he is a new creature: old things are passed away; behold, all things are become new. "

Those that are written in the Lamb's Book of Life are what the Bible calls the "overcomers" and are more than "conquerors" in Christ Jesus. Only those people that belong to this group are able to resist the devil and can never be deceived no matter what comes and goes.

"For there shall arise false Christs, and false prophets, and shall shew great signs and wonders; insomuch that, if it were possible, they shall deceive the very elect." (Matt. 24:24). The elect can never be deceived because their names are written in the Lamb's Book of Life.

That is also stated in Revelation 17:8, *"The BEAST that thou* sawest was, and is not; and shall ascend out of the bottomless pit, and go into perdition: and they that dwell on the earth shall wonder, whose NAMES were NOT written in the BOOK of LIFE from the foundation of the world... " "And ALL that dwell upon the earth shall worship him (the Beast), whose NAMES are NOT written in the BOOK of LIFE of the LAMB SLAIN from the FOUNDATION of the world" *(Revelations 13:8).*

A RECORD OF NAMES:

L et it be known that there is NOT ONE Scripture that teaches that God is presently compiling a record of names.

This has already been done before the foundation of the world.

Also, it is not a question of simply involving ourselves with two groups of people both of whom had opportunity to receive eternal life, wherein one group received it and had their names placed on record while the others who refused did not have their names so placed.

And now notice that, there is a group of people whose names having already been placed on that record before the foundation of the world, CANNOT UNDER ANY CIRCUMSTANCES BE REMOVED; and there is another group WHOSE NAMES WERE ON THAT RECORD BEFORE THE FOUNDATION OF THE WORLD BUT WILL HAVE THEIR NAMES REMOVED.

The following is an account of the six different types of people in the records of God:

THE TRUE SABBATH THAT WAS PROMISED IS YOUR TRUE REST IN CHRIST JESUS:

We shall use scripture to answer scripture, and may God grants us the revelation for the letter killeth but the spirit giveth life.

Genesis 2:1-3 KJV

Thus the heavens and the earth were finished, and all the host of them.

And on the seventh day, God ended his work which he had made; and he rested on the seventh day from all his work which he had made.

And God blessed the seventh day and sanctified it: because that in it he had rested from all his work which God created and made.

Exodus 20:8-11. KJV

Remember the sabbath day, to keep it holy.

Six days shalt thou labor, and do all thy work: 10 But the seventh day is the sabbath of the Lord thy God: in it, thou shalt not do any work, thou, nor thy son, nor thy daughter, thy manservant, nor thy maidservant, nor thy cattle, nor thy stranger that is within thy gates: 11 For in six days the Lord made heaven and earth, the sea, and all that in them is, and rested the seventh day: wherefore the Lord blessed the sabbath day and hallowed it.

Numbers 15:32-35. KJV

And while the children of Israel were in the wilderness, they found a man that gathered sticks upon the sabbath day.

And they that found him gathering sticks brought him unto Moses and Aaron, and unto all the congregation. And they put him in ward because it was not declared what should be done to him. And the LORD said unto Moses, The man shall be surely put to death: all the congregation shall stone him with stones without the camp.

Hebrews 4:1-13. Let us, therefore, fear, lest, a promise being left us of entering into his rest, any of you should seem to come short of it. For unto us was the gospel preached, as well as unto them: but the word preached did not profit them, not being mixed with faith in them that heard it.

For we which have believed do enter into rest, as he said, As I have sworn in my wrath if they shall enter into my rest: although the works were finished from the foundation of the world.

For he spake in a certain place of the seventh day on this wise, And God did rest the seventh day from all his works.

And in this place again, If they shall enter into my rest.

Seeing, therefore, it remaineth that some must enter therein, and they to whom it was first preached entered not in because of unbelief: Again, he limiteth a certain day, saying in David, today, after so long a time; as it is said, Today if ye will hear his voice, harden not your hearts.

For if Jesus had given them rest, then would he not afterward have spoken of another day. There remaineth, therefore, a rest to the people of God.

For he that is entered into his rest, he also hath ceased from his own works, as God did from his. Let us labor, therefore, to enter into that rest, lest any man fall after the same example of unbelief.

For the word of God is quick, and powerful, and sharper than any two-edged sword, piercing even to the dividing asunder of soul and spirit, and of the joints and marrow, and is a discerner of the thoughts and intents of the heart.

Neither is there any creature that is not manifest in his sight: but all things are naked and opened unto the eyes of him with whom we have to do, the congregation shall stone him with stones without the camp.

Jesus said, in Matthew 11:28-29 KJV.

[28]Come unto me, all ye that labor and are heavy laden, and I will give you rest.

[29]Take my yoke upon you and learn of me; for I am meek and lowly in heart: and ye shall find rest unto your souls.

IT WAS ON THE DAY OF PENTECOST WHEN THEY WERE ALL FILLED WITH THE HOLY GHOST IS THE TRUE SABBATH THAT WAS PROMISED. THUS, WHEN THEY WERE FILLED WITH THE HOLY GHOST THEY CEASED FROM THEIR WORLDLY WORKS, THEIR WORLDLY DOINGS, THEIR SECRET LIVES AND STRUGGLES OF CARNALITIES AND EVIL WAYS.

THE HOLY GHOST TOOK CHARGE AND CONTROL OF THEIR LIVES. THERE, THEY ENTERED THEIR REST, WAITING FOR THEIR MILLENNIAL REIGN, OH GLORY TO GOD, AMEN. YOU MUST BE BORN AGAIN AND RECEIVE THE HOLY GHOST AND ENTER INTO YOUR REST. There is your rest!

The Holy Ghost is your Sabbath, that is your rest. IT IS NOT A CERTAIN DAY, NOR A CERTAIN YEAR, BUT ETERNITY OF BEING FILLED AND BLESSED IN THE HOLY SPIRIT. It is you ceasing from all your secret sins and struggles of the flesh, and God doing. It is God in you willing and doing of His good pleasure. You being a written epistle read of all men. It is your conversion and new birth, it's your testimony and Christ in you the hope of glory.

NOW ACCORDING TO THE HEBREW CALENDAR AND TRADITIONAL CHRISTIAN CALENDERS, SUNDAY, IS THE FIRST DAY OF THE WEEK.

The observers of Saturday for Sabbath are ignorant of the fact that the disciples worshipped or assembled on Sundays.

Acts 20:7. KJV

> 7 And upon the first day of the week, when the disciples came together to break bread, Paul preached unto them, ready to depart on the morrow; and continued his speech until midnight.

1 Corinthians 16:2 KJV.

Upon the first day of the week let every
one of you lay by him in store, as God hath
prospered him, that there be no gatherings
when I come.

One point is here plainly proved. Many tell us that the
Sabbath command is merely for "one day in seven"—that
it does not have to be the seventh day of the week, but
merely the seventh part of time. They argue that Sunday,
being one day out of seven, fulfills the command. But this
passage states in plain language that, three days after all
abolished things had been done away, the Sabbath still
existed and that it was the seventh day of the week. But
was the day changed later?

1. Mark 16:2: "Very early in the morning, on the first
   day of the week, they came to the tomb when the
   sun had risen."

This first day of the week was, according to verse 1,
"when the Sabbath was past."

2. Mark 16:9: "Now when He rose [was risen, KJV]
   early on the first day of the week, He appeared first
   to Mary Magdalene, out of whom He had cast seven
   demons." This text, poorly translated, speaks of Jesus'
   appearance to Mary Magdalene later the same day

3. John 20:1: "On the first day of the week Mary
   Magdalene came to the tomb early, while it was still
   dark..." This, written more than sixty years after the

crucifixion, is merely John's version, describing the same visit to the tomb. It confirms the facts above.

4. John 20:19: "Then, the same day at evening, being the first day of the week, when the doors were shut where the disciples were assembled, for fear of the Jews, Jesus came and stood in the midst, and said to them, 'Peace be with you.'" Let us examine this carefully, for some claim this was a religious service called to celebrate the resurrection.

Notice, it was Jesus' first opportunity to appear to His disciples. For three and a half years, He had been constantly with them, on all days of the week. His meeting with them, of itself, could not establish Saturday as a Sabbath.

Were they meeting together to celebrate the resurrection, thus establishing Sunday as the Christian Sabbath in honor of the resurrection? Therefore, neither Saturday nor Sunday is their REST.

Nothing in this text calls this day the "Sabbath," the "Lord's Day," or any sacred title. Nothing here sets it apart or makes it holy. Scripture gives no authority here for changing a command of God!

5. Acts 20:7: "Now on the first day of the week, when the disciples came together to break bread, Paul, ready to depart the next day, spoke to them and continued his message until midnight." Here, at last, we find a religious meeting on the first day of the week, the disciples always held communion

every first day of the week. It simply relates the events of this one particular first day of the week.

That "the disciples came together to break bread" means that they gathered to eat a meal. This expression was commonly used to designate a meal in past times. Luke 24:30; Acts 2:46; 27:35 for further examples of "breaking bread.

Our Lord Jesus Christ declared Himself to be "The Lord of the Sabbath". Not one time did He place emphasis on the keeping of a Saturday Sabbath. On the contrary, instead of pointing them to the Seventh-day Sabbath, He pointed to Himself saying, "...come unto me and I will give you "rest.""

In His teachings, Jesus was endeavoring to move them away from the emphasis they were placing on the Seventh-day Sabbath and their claim to being Abraham's seed because of "physical" circumcision. Jesus would take circumcision and the Sabbath out of the "physical" realm and place it in a "spiritual" realm. He would ask us to remember and keep holy that Sabbath (rest) which is in honor of God's

"New" Creation, by a New Birth. The Old Creation is under God's judgment and will pass away, BUT this New Creation is Eternal. "For in Christ Jesus neither circumcision availeth anything nor uncircumcision, but a new creation."

(Galatians 6;15).

The New Testament places "no emphasis" on the keeping of a Seventh-day Sabbath, but it places tremendous emphasis on the "faith of Abraham", encouraging us to follow his example.

> 6. I Corinthians 16:2: "On the first day of the week let each one of you lay something aside, storing up as he may prosper that there be no collections when I come." Often we see this text printed on the little offering envelopes in the pews of Churches, and many preach that this text sets Sunday as the time for taking up the church collection for doing God's work and paying the minister and church expenses.

Verse 1 tells us what kind of collection is being made: "Now concerning the collection for the saints, as I have given orders to the Churches of Galatia, so you must do also. "First, it is a collection—not for the preacher, evangelism, or church expenses—but "for the saints." The members of the church in Jerusalem were suffering from drought and famine. They needed, not money, but food.

Notice that Paul had given similar instruction to other Churches. He tells the Romans: "And when I come, whomever you approve by your letters I will send to bear your gift to Jerusalem. But if it is fitting that I go also, they [more than one] will go with me" (verses 3-4). Apparently, it was going to require several men to carry this collection, gathered and stored up, to Jerusalem. Thus, once again, the first day of the week is a Sunday.

The Bible says: "the natural man cannot receive the things of the Spirit of God...neither can he know them because they are "spiritually discerned" (1st. Cor. 2:14). God had worked for six days, and now He rested. The question now should be, "What kind of "Rest" did God enter into? Is God tired?

This rest in Genesis 2:2-3, was not physical, because God is never tired. "He fainteth not, neither is weary" (Isaiah 40:28).

So, what is the meaning of "His rest"? It signifies God's satisfaction with His creation. All who study the Scriptures carefully should understand the meaning of God's rest.

After God had finished His works, He rested in the Eternal day which is always day and never night. For God, this Seventh-day rest blended into Eternity from whence He came to make His creation.

In Genesis 2:2-3, it shows that God is planting a spiritual "seed" which was destined, in the New Testament, to "blossom" into a "New Birth" with a Resurrection, Rapture, Millennium, and complete Eternal Sabbath "Rest" for all "His" children.

Therefore, we can see that God's True Sabbath was made flesh in the person of Jesus Christ, but the Jews rejected It (John 1:14). He came onto His own and they knew Him not. He was both "The Lord of the Sabbath" and "The Sabbath of the Lord". He was and is God's "Everlasting Sign" to His children; Not a Seventh-day Sabbath, but a Sabbath-Rest in the Lord of the Sabbath, Our Lord Jesus Christ.

We have already said that in our earlier deposition as found in our study that, the New Testament, the emphasis is placed, NOT on "physical" circumcision BUT on "Spiritual" circumcision.

We also found that, in the New Testament, the emphasis is placed on the keeping of a "Spiritual" Sabbath rest in Christ, and NOT a physical Seventh-day Sabbath, which first came to the Jews and the Gentiles.

Have you experienced the "rest" and "refreshing" found in God's True Sabbath? If you will allow Him, the Lord Jesus will, through Acts 2:37-39 guide you into His Sabbath Rest.

Act on the instructions given to those first believers and you too shall receive the "Gift of God's Sabbath Rest".

Here in Isaiah (quoted above), 700 years before it came to pass, God prophesied of His coming "New Sabbath"; Not "a" day (evening and morning), but an experience in Christ, through the infilling of the Holy Ghost.

On the Day of Pentecost (the first day of the week - Sunday), 700 years after the prophecy, God manifested His True Sabbath. Thus when they were filled with the Holy Ghost they ceased from their worldly works, their worldly doings, their evil ways, and ceased trying to establish their own righteousness. The Holy Spirit took control of their lives. They entered into "rest".

There is your "rest". That is your Sabbath. It is you ceasing, and God, through the Holy Spirit, doing. It is God in you willing and doing of His good pleasure. Blessed indeed is the man and woman who can "remember this Sabbath and keep it holy" every day.

Truly, As a New Creature in Christ Jesus, it is not I who keeps the Sabbath, but the Sabbath keeps me. It isn't keeping Sunday or keeping Saturday, it's entering into and remaining in Christ every day. Worship on Sunday serves only as an "a memorial" of the resurrection and of the Sabbath Rest we have found in Christ.

Therefore, those who observe a Saturday Sabbath, are actually "in their works" denying the resurrection of Jesus Christ. "This is indeed a hard saying. Who can receive it?

So what the Jews did as Sabbath was just a shadow of the real rest. They worked, rested and went back to work again in a continual cycle. This is not what God did.

Thus the "works" here do not refer to our works whereby we earn a living. It has a deeper meaning. "Our own works" refer to our sinful works that must cease. We are born sinners and do our own works. "Our own works" also refer to our own ambitions and agendas and interests. God wants us to be a part of His plans, not our own plans.

Colossians 2:16

Let no man, therefore, judge you in meat, or in drink, or in respect of a holy day, or of the new moon, or of the SABBATH days:

[17] Which are a shadow of things to come; but the body is of Christ.

Our real burden is sin. We need Jesus to wash away our sins and unbelief. Then we can rest in Him.

NOW ACCORDING TO THE HEBREW CALENDAR AND TRADITIONAL CHRISTIAN

CALENDERS, SUNDAY, IS THE FIRST DAY OF THE WEEK.

The observers of Saturday for Sabbath, are ignorant of the fact that the disciples worshipped or assembled on Sundays.

Acts 20:7. KJV

> [7]And upon the first day of the week, when the disciples came together to break bread, Paul preached unto them, ready to depart on the morrow; and continued his speech until midnight.

> Corinthians 16:2 KJV. Upon the first day of the week let every one of you lay by him in store, as God hath prospered him, that there be no gatherings when I come.

One point is here plainly proved. Many tell us that the Sabbath command is merely for "one day in seven"—that it does not have to be the seventh day of the week, but merely the seventh part of the time. They argue that Sunday, being one day out of seven, fulfills the command. But this passage states in plain language that, three days after all abolished things had been done away, the Sabbath still existed and that it was the seventh day of the week. But was the day changed later?

1. Mark 16:2: "Very early in the morning, on the first day of the week, they came to the tomb when the sun had risen."

This first day of the week was, according to verse 1, "when the Sabbath was past."

2. . Mark 16:9: "Now when He rose [was risen, KJV] early on the first day of the week, He appeared first to Mary Magdalene, out of whom He had cast seven demons." This text, poorly translated, speaks of Jesus' appearance to Mary Magdalene later the same day

3. John 20:1: "On the first day of the week Mary Magdalene came to the tomb early, while it was still dark" This, written more than sixty years after the crucifixion, is merely John's version, describing the same visit to the tomb. It confirms the facts above.

4. John 20:19: "Then, the same day at evening, being the first day of the week, when the doors were shut where the disciples were assembled, for fear of the Jews, Jesus came and stood in the midst, and said to them, 'Peace be with you.'" Let us examine this carefully, for some claim this was a religious service called to celebrate the resurrection.

Notice, it was Jesus' first opportunity to appear to His disciples. For three and a half years, He had been constantly with them, on all days of the week. His meeting with them, of itself, could not establish Saturday as a Sabbath.

Were they meeting together to celebrate the resurrection, thus establishing Sunday as the Christian Sabbath in honor of the resurrection? Therefore, neither Saturday nor Sunday is their REST. Nothing in this text calls this day the "Sabbath," the "Lord's Day," or any sacred title. Nothing here sets it apart or makes it holy. Scripture gives no authority here for changing a command of God!

5. Acts 20:7: "Now on the first day of the week, when the disciples came together to break bread, Paul, ready to depart the next day, spoke to them and continued his message until midnight." Here, at last, we find a religious meeting on the first day of the week, the disciples always held communion every first day of the week. It simply relates the events of this one particular first day of the week.

That "the disciples came together to break bread" means that they gathered to eat a meal. This expression was commonly used to designate a meal in past times. Luke 24:30; Acts 2:46; 27:35 for further examples of "breaking bread.

6. I Corinthians 16:2: "On the first day of the week let each one of you lay something aside, storing up as he may prosper that there be no collections when I come." Often we see this text printed on the little offering envelopes in the pews of Churches, and many preach that this text sets Sunday as the time for taking up the church collection for doing God's work and paying the minister and church expenses.

Verse 1 tells us what kind of collection is being made: "Now concerning the collection for the saints, as I have given orders to the Churches of Galatia, so you must do also." First, it is a collection—not for the preacher, evangelism, or church expenses—but "for the saints." The members of the church in Jerusalem were suffering from drought and famine. They needed, not money, but food.

Notice that Paul had given similar instruction to other Churches. He tells the Romans: "And when I come, whomever you approve by your letters I will send to bear your gift to Jerusalem. But if it is fitting that I go also, they [more than one] will go with me" (verses 3-4). Apparently, it was going to require several men to carry this collection, gathered and stored up, to Jerusalem. Thus, once again, the first day of the week is a Sunday.

THE TRUE SABBATH THAT WAS PROMISED:

That is exactly your rest in CHRIST JESUS: GEN 2:1-3: We shall use scripture to answer scripture, and may God grant us the revelation for the letter killeth but the spirit giveth life.

Genesis 2:1-3 KJV

Thus the heavens and the earth were finished, and all the host of them. And on the seventh day, God ended his work which he had made; and he rested on the seventh day from all his work which he had made.

And God blessed the seventh day and sanctified it: because that in it he had rested from all his work which God created and made.

Exodus 20:8-11. KJV

Remember the sabbath day, to keep it holy.

Six days shalt thou labor, and do all thy work: 10 But the seventh day is the sabbath of the Lord thy God: in it, thou shalt not do any work, thou, nor thy son, nor thy daughter, thy manservant, nor thy maidservant, nor thy cattle, nor thy stranger that is within thy gates:

For in six days the Lord made heaven and earth, the sea, and all that in them is, and rested the seventh day: wherefore the Lord blessed the sabbath day, and hallowed it.

Numbers 15:32-35. KJV

And while the children of Israel were in the wilderness, they found a man that gathered sticks upon the sabbath day.

And they that found him gathering sticks brought him unto Moses and Aaron, and unto all the congregation. And they put him in ward because it was not declared what should be done to him. And the LORD said unto Moses, The man shall be surely put to death: all the congregation shall stone him with stones without the camp.

Hebrews 4:1-13. Let us, therefore, fear, lest a promise being left us of entering into his rest, any of you should seem to come short of it. For unto us was the gospel preached, as well as unto them: but the word preached did not profit them, not being mixed with faith in them that heard it.

For we which have believed do enter into rest, as he said, As I have sworn in my wrath if they shall enter into my rest: although the works were finished from the foundation of the world.

For he spake in a certain place of the seventh day on this wise, And God did rest the seventh day from all his works.

And in this place again, If they shall enter into my rest.

Seeing, therefore, it remaineth that some must enter therein, and they to whom it was first preached entered not in because of unbelief: Again, he limiteth a certain day, saying in David, today, after so long a time; as it is said, Today if ye will hear his voice, harden not your hearts.

For if Jesus had given them rest, then would he not afterward have spoken of another day. There remaineth, therefore, a rest to the people of God.

For he that is entered into his rest, he also hath ceased from his own works, as God did from his. Let us labor, therefore, to enter into that rest, lest any man fall after the same example of unbelief.

For the word of God is quick, and powerful, and sharper than any two-edged sword, piercing even to the dividing asunder of soul and spirit, and of the joints and marrow, and is a discerner of the thoughts and intents of the heart.

Neither is there any creature that is not manifest in his sight: but all things are naked and opened unto the eyes of him with whom we have to do, the congregation shall stone him with stones without the camp.

Jesus said, in Matthew 11:28-29 KJV. 28 Come unto me, all ye that labor and are heavy laden, and I will give you rest.

29 Take my yoke upon you and learn of me; for I am meek and lowly in heart: and ye shall find rest unto your souls.

IT WAS ON THE DAY OF PENTECOST WHEN THEY WERE ALL FILLED WITH THE HOLY GHOST IS THE TRUE SABBATH THAT WAS PROMISED. THUS, WHEN THEY WERE FILLED WITH THE HOLY GHOST THEY CEASED FROM

THEIR WORLDLY WORKS, THEIR WORLDLY DOINGS, THEIR SECRET LIVES AND STRUGGLES OF CARNALITIES AND EVIL WAYS.

THE HOLY GHOST TOOK CHARGE AND CONTROL OF THEIR LIVES. THERE, THEY ENTERED THEIR REST, WAITING FOR THEIR MILLENNIAL REIGN, OH GLORY TO GOD, AMEN. YOU MUST BE BORN AGAIN AND RECEIVE THE HOLY GHOST AND ENTER INTO YOUR REST. There is your rest!

The Holy Ghost is your Sabbath, that is your rest. IT IS NOT A CERTAIN DAY, NOR A CERTAIN YEAR, BUT ETERNITY OF BEING FILLED AND BLESSED IN THE HOLY SPIRIT. It is you ceasing from all your secret sins and struggles of the flesh, and God doing. It is God in you willing and doing of His good pleasure. You being a written epistle read of all men. It is your conversion and new birth, it's your testimony and Christ in you the hope of glory.

NOW ACCORDING TO THE HEBREW CALENDAR AND TRADITIONAL CHRISTIAN CALENDERS, SUNDAY, IS THE FIRST DAY OF THE WEEK.

The observers of Saturday for Sabbath, are ignorant of the fact that the disciples worshipped or assembled on Sundays.

Acts 20:7. KJV

7 And upon the first day of the week, when the disciples came together to break bread, Paul preached

unto them, ready to depart on the morrow; and continued his speech until midnight.

Corinthians 16:2 KJV. Upon the first day of the week let every one of you lay by him in store, as God hath prospered him, that there be no gatherings when I come.

One point is here plainly proved. Many tell us that the Sabbath command is merely for "one day in seven"—that it does not have to be the seventh day of the week, but merely the seventh part of time. They argue that Sunday, being one day out of seven, fulfills the command. But this passage states in plain language that, three days after all abolished things had been done away, the Sabbath still existed and that it was the seventh day of the week. But was the day changed later?

1. Mark 16:2: "Very early in the morning, on the first day of the week, they came to the tomb when the sun had risen."

This first day of the week was, according to verse 1, "when the Sabbath was past."

2. Mark 16:9: "Now when He rose [was risen, KJV] early on the first day of the week, He appeared first to Mary Magdalene, out of whom He had cast seven demons." This text, poorly translated, speaks of Jesus' appearance to Mary Magdalene later the same day

3. John 20:1: "On the first day of the week Mary Magdalene came to the tomb early, while it was still dark" This, written more than

sixty years after the crucifixion, is merely John's version, describing the same visit to the tomb. It confirms the facts above.

4. John 20:19: "Then, the same day at evening, being the first day of the week, when the doors were shut where the disciples were assembled, for fear of the Jews, Jesus came and stood in the midst, and said to them, 'Peace be with you.'" Let us examine this carefully, for some claim this was a religious service called to celebrate the resurrection.

Notice, it was Jesus' first opportunity to appear to His disciples.

For three and a half years, He had been constantly with them, on all days of the week. His meeting with them, of itself, could not establish Saturday as a Sabbath.

Were they meeting together to celebrate the resurrection, thus establishing Sunday as the Christian Sabbath in honor of the resurrection? Therefore, neither Saturday nor Sunday is their REST. Nothing in this text calls this day the "Sabbath," the "Lord's Day," or any sacred title. Nothing here sets it apart or makes it holy. Scripture gives no authority here for changing a command of God!

5. Acts 20:7: "Now on the first day of the week, when the disciples came together to break bread, Paul, ready to depart the next day, spoke to them and continued his message until midnight." Here, at last, we find a religious meeting on the first day of the week, the disciples always held communion

every first day of the week? It simply relates the events of this one particular first day of the week.

That "the disciples came together to break bread" means that they gathered to eat a meal. This expression was commonly used to designate a meal in past times. Luke 24:30; Acts 2:46; 27:35 for further examples of "breaking bread.

Our Lord Jesus Christ declared Himself to be "The Lord of the Sabbath". Not one time did He place emphasis on the keeping of a Saturday Sabbath. On the contrary, instead of pointing them to the Seventh-day Sabbath, He pointed to Himself saying, "...come unto me and I will give you "rest.""

In His teachings, Jesus was endeavoring to move them away from the emphasis they were placing on the Seventh-day Sabbath and their claim to being Abraham's seed because of "physical" circumcision. Jesus would take circumcision and the Sabbath out of the "physical" realm and place it in a "spiritual" realm. He would ask us to remember and keep holy that Sabbath (rest) which is in honor of God's

"New" Creation, by a New Birth. The Old Creation is under God's judgment and will pass away, BUT this New Creation is Eternal. "For in Christ Jesus neither circumcision availeth anything nor uncircumcision, but a new creation."

(Galatians 6;15).

The New Testament places "no emphasis" on the keeping of a Seventh-day Sabbath, but it places tremendous emphasis on the "faith of Abraham", encouraging us to follow his example.

6. I Corinthians 16:2: "On the first day of the week let each one of you lay something aside, storing up as he may prosper that there be no collections when I come." Often we see this text printed on the little offering envelopes in the pews of Churches, and many preach that this text sets Sunday as the time for taking up the church collection for doing God's work and paying the minister and church expenses.

Verse 1 tells us what kind of collection is being made: "Now concerning the collection for the saints, as I have given orders to the Churches of Galatia, so you must do also." First, it is a collection—not for the preacher, evangelism, or church expenses—but "for the saints." The members of the church in Jerusalem were suffering from drought and famine. They needed, not money, but food.

Notice that Paul had given similar instruction to other Churches. He tells the Romans: "And when I come, whomever you approve by your letters I will send to bear your gift to Jerusalem. But if it is fitting that I go also, they [more than one] will go with me" (verses 3-4). Apparently, it was going to require several men to carry this collection, gathered and stored up, to Jerusalem. Thus, once again, the first day of the week is a Sunday.

The Bible says: "the natural man cannot receive the things of the Spirit of God...neither can he know them because they are "spiritually discerned" (1st. Cor. 2:14).

God had worked for six days, and now He rested. The question now should be, "What kind of "Rest" did God enter into? Is God tired?

This rest in Genesis 2:2-3, was not physical, because God is never tired. "He fainteth not, neither is weary" (Isaiah 40:28).

So what is the meaning of "His rest"? It signifies God's satisfaction with His creation. All who study the Scriptures carefully should understand the meaning of God's rest.

After God had finished His works, He rested in the Eternal day which is always day and never night. For God, this Seventh-day rest blended into Eternity from whence He came to make His creation.

In Genesis 2:2-3, it shows that God is planting a spiritual "seed" which was destined, in the New Testament, to "blossom" into a "New Birth" with a Resurrection, Rapture, Millennium, and complete Eternal Sabbath "Rest" for all "His" children.

Therefore, we can see that God's True Sabbath was made flesh in the person of Jesus Christ, but the Jews rejected It (John 1:14). He came onto His own and they knew Him not. He was both "The Lord of the Sabbath" and "The Sabbath of the Lord". He was and is God's "Everlasting Sign" to His children; Not a Seventh-day Sabbath, but a Sabbath-Rest in the Lord of the Sabbath, Our Lord Jesus Christ.

We have already said that in our earlier deposition as found in our study that, the New Testament, the emphasis is placed, NOT on "physical" circumcision BUT on "Spiritual" circumcision.

We also found that, in the New Testament, the emphasis is placed on the keeping of a "Spiritual" Sabbath rest in Christ, and NOT a physical Seventh-day Sabbath, which first came to the Jews and the Gentiles.

Have you experienced the "rest" and "refreshing" found in God's True Sabbath? If you will allow Him, the Lord Jesus will, through Acts 2:37-39 guide you into His Sabbath Rest.

Act on the instructions given to those first believers and you too shall receive the "Gift of God's Sabbath Rest".

Here in Isaiah (quoted above), 700 years before it came to pass, God prophesied of His coming "New Sabbath"; Not "a" day (evening and morning), but an experience in Christ, through the infilling of the Holy Ghost.

On the Day of Pentecost (the first day of the week - Sunday), 700 years after the prophecy, God manifested His True Sabbath. Thus when they were filled with the Holy Ghost they ceased from their worldly works, their worldly doings, their evil ways, and ceased trying to establish their own righteousness. The Holy Spirit took control of their lives. They entered into "rest".

There is your "rest". That is your Sabbath. It is you ceasing, and God, through the Holy Spirit, doing. It is God in you willing and doing of His good pleasure. Blessed indeed is the man and woman who can "remember this Sabbath and keep it holy" every day.

Truly, As a New Creature in Christ Jesus, it is not I who keeps the Sabbath, but the Sabbath keeps me. It isn't keeping Sunday or keeping Saturday, it's entering into and remaining in Christ every day. Worship on Sunday serves only as an "a memorial" of the resurrection and of the Sabbath Rest we have found in Christ.

Therefore, those who observe a Saturday Sabbath, are actually "in their works" denying the resurrection of Jesus Christ. "This is indeed a hard saying. Who can receive it?

So what the Jews did as Sabbath was just a shadow of the real rest. They worked, rested and went back to work again in a continual cycle. This is not what God did.

Thus the "works" here do not refer to our works whereby we earn a living. It has a deeper meaning. "Our own works" refer to our sinful works that must cease. We are born sinners and do our own works. "Our own works" also refer to our own ambitions and agendas and interests. God wants us to be a part of His plans, not our own plans.

Colossians 2:16

Let no man, therefore, judge you in meat, or in drink, or in respect of a holy day, or of the new moon, or of the SABBATH days:

[17] Which are a shadow of things to come; but the body is of Christ.

Our real burden is sin. We need Jesus to wash away our sins and unbelief. Then we can rest in Him.

NOW ACCORDING TO THE HEBREW CALENDAR AND TRADITIONAL CHRISTIAN

CALENDERS, SUNDAY, IS THE FIRST DAY OF THE WEEK.

The observers of Saturday for Sabbath, are ignorant of the fact that the disciples worshipped or assembled on Sundays.

Acts 20:7. KJV

⁷ And upon the first day of the week, when the disciples came together to break bread, Paul preached unto them, ready to depart on the morrow; and continued his speech until midnight.

Corinthians 16:2 KJV. Upon the first day of the week let every one of you lay by him in store, as God hath prospered him, that there be no gatherings when I come.

One point is here plainly proved. Many tell us that the Sabbath command is merely for "one day in seven"— that it does not have to be the seventh day of the week, but merely the seventh part of the time. They argue that Sunday, being one day out of seven, fulfills the command. But this passage states in plain language that, three days after all abolished things had been done away, the Sabbath still existed and that it was the seventh day of the week. But was the day changed later?

1. Mark 16:2: "Very early in the morning, on the first day of the week, they came to the tomb when the sun had risen."

This first day of the week was, according to verse 1, "when the Sabbath was past."

2. Mark 16:9: "Now when He rose [was risen, KJV] early on the first day of the week, He appeared first to Mary Magdalene, out of whom He had cast seven demons." This text, poorly translated, speaks of Jesus' appearance to Mary Magdalene later the same day

3. John 20:1: "On the first day of the week Mary Magdalene came to the tomb early, while it was still dark " This, written more than

sixty years after the crucifixion, is merely John's version, describing the same visit to the tomb. It confirms the facts above.

4. John 20:19: "Then, the same day at evening, being the first day of the week, when the doors were shut where the disciples were assembled, for fear of the Jews, Jesus came and stood in the midst, and said to them, 'Peace be with you.'" Let us examine this carefully, for some claim this was a religious service called to celebrate the resurrection.

Notice, it was Jesus' first opportunity to appear to His disciples. For three and a half years, He had been constantly with them, on all days of the week. His meeting with them, of itself, could not establish Saturday as a Sabbath.

Were they meeting together to celebrate the resurrection, thus establishing Sunday as the Christian Sabbath in honor of the resurrection? Therefore, neither Saturday nor Sunday is their REST. Nothing in this text calls this day the "Sabbath," the "Lord's Day," or any sacred title. Nothing here sets it apart or makes it holy. Scripture gives no authority here for changing a command of God!

5. Acts 20:7: "Now on the first day of the week, when the disciples came together to break bread, Paul, ready to depart the next day, spoke to them and continued his message until midnight." Here, at last, we find a religious meeting on the first day of the week, the disciples always held communion every first day of the week? It simply relates the events of this one particular first day of the week.

That "the disciples came together to break bread" means that they gathered to eat a meal. This expression was commonly used to designate a meal in past times. Luke 24:30; Acts 2:46; 27:35 for further examples of "breaking bread.

6. I Corinthians 16:2: "On the first day of the week let each one of you lay something aside, storing up as he may prosper that there be no collections when I come." Often we see this text printed on the little offering envelopes in the pews of Churches, and many preach that this text sets Sunday as the time for taking up the church collection for doing God's work and paying the minister and church expenses.

Verse 1 tells us what kind of collection is being made: "Now concerning the collection for the saints, as I have given orders to the Churches of Galatia, so you must do also. "First, it is a collection—not for the preacher, evangelism, or church expenses—but "for the saints." The members of the church in Jerusalem were suffering from drought and famine. They needed, not money, but food.

Notice that Paul had given similar instruction to other Churches. He tells the Romans: "And when I come, whomever you approve by your letters I will send to bear your gift to Jerusalem. But if it is fitting that I go also, they [more than one] will go with me" (verses 3-4). Apparently, it was going to require several men to carry this collection, gathered and stored up, to Jerusalem. Thus, once again, the first day of the week is a Sunday.

DISTRIBUTION:

"This book is intended for your in-depth knowledge of God's Word and revelation. It is believed that you obtain help by prayerfully and diligently studying to equip yourself with the basic fundamental truth of the Gospel of our Lord Christ I hereby strongly recommend that you grab you're a copy of this incisive, revealing booklet online, through the amazon, ebay, google, barnesandnoble, major bookstores etc, Libraries and Churches.

Win a soul for Christ today, with a copy for yourself, new converts, loved ones, and this gospel of the Kingdom shall be preached to the uttermost parts of the world and the end shall come.

CONTACT US:

Bro CALEB IWORIE
Email: Seedwordoutreach@gmail.com
Pastor ZOE DEMBE
Email: Houstontabernacle@gmail.com
Houston Tabernacle, 6104 Westline Drive, Houston, Texas 77036.